Affirmation for Wa

MW00931487

"Michael did what Grandfather had hoped people of all religions and faiths would do with his spiritual teachings, and that is to integrate them into their own lives, empowering their own faith, and going beyond what they thought was spiritually possible. In *Walking with Grandfather* I can so clearly see the fit, the mesh, and the fine fabric of bringing together what Grandfather had taught and what Michael has lived into a new reality where taking the simple beliefs of Grandfather helps us understand fully what we embrace and believe. God bless you Michael for your wonderful, enlightening, and highly inspirational book that I hope will go on to help so many others."

Tom Brown Jr., Founder of The Tracker School and author of *The Tracker*, *The Journey* and *Awakening Spirits*

"*Walking with Grandfather* is a true conversion experience almost too profound for words, except that Michael does exactly that—he writes a beautifully moving, deeply spiritual, hysterically funny, and vitally important story of his walk with Grandfather. He will make you laugh and cry and shake your head in both wonder and disbelief. But more importantly, Michael's story will motivate you to contemplate an image of Jesus that takes discipleship to new levels of faith and commitment, that has a significant impact on the power of prayer, and that helps us realize our intimate connection with God, each other, and all of creation. So set aside your certainty and your skepticism and take this walk with Michael Hardin. You will never again see the world or the God who created it in the same way."

Sharon Baker, Associate Professor of Religion, Messiah College, Author of *Executing God*

"Michael Hardin's *Walking with Grandfather* is a beautifully written and heartfelt chronicle of the author's journey from despair to hope. In an era scarred by violent fundamentalism and destructive consumerism, Hardin articulates the Earth-centered religious values and practices that are essential for healthy, mindful living. Visionary thinkers René Girard, Karl Barth, and Tom Brown Jr. are Hardin's traveling companions in his personal odyssey. A stunning achievement and must read for students and scholars interested in biblically-centered sustainable living as an answer to the loss of hope in our time."

Mark Wallace, Professor, Dept. of Religion, Swarthmore College, Author of *Finding God if the Singing River*

"*'The road to wholeness,*" wrote Jung, "*is made up of fateful detours and wrong turnings.*' Hardin relates a journey that includes an abusive childhood and struggles with addiction, a swing from Christian fundamentalism to agnostic biblical scholarship, a failed pastorate and the road to recovery. His study—at first reluctantly, then devotedly--with renowned tracker Tom Brown Jr., helps Hardin recover his faith and vocation through reconnecting with Creation. Both skeptic and acolyte, Hardin explores how a Christian path can converge peaceably and fruitfully with a deep spirituality of nature—a welcome testimony in our world of culture wars and dualistic antagonisms."

Ched Myers, Activist and Author of *Binding the Strong Man*

"It is difficult to describe Michael Hardin's *Walking with Grandfather*. It is part searingly honest biography, part an account of comical misadventures in the wilderness, part introduction to Native American spiritual practices, and part introduction to the works of René Girard and Karl Barth. Through it all is a plea for awareness--a plea to see the world, creation in its glory and pain and to connect what may appear to be abstruse theology with the grimy realities of life in our broken world. This is a book as compelling, moving and outrageous as Michael himself! It draws us out of ourselves, our heads, to encounter God who lives in and through the created order and through the incarnate Christ."

John E. Phelan, Senior Professor of Theological Studies,
North Park Theological Seminary

"More and more of us, educated to the hilt in the institutions of modernity, are discovering that there are other approaches to wisdom that enrich our lives and engage our moral sensibilities. Often, those alternative approaches come from non-Western or pre-modern sources. Here, Michael Hardin, a "failed fundamentalist" with a PhD, shares the story - sometimes humorous, sometimes raucous, sometimes reverent - of his encounter with wisdom from a rich Native American tradition."

Brian D. McLaren, Author of
We Make the Road by Walking

"Here you have it: the true confessions and surprising faith (the tears and prayers) of Michael Hardin. You might not believe what you read here—or like it—but in Michael's case, that was a superb place to start! Be a skeptic. Then see how sin and grace, life and love can make you a convinced skeptic. For Hardin's readers, this book will answer many questions and raise even more. If so, you're walking as he has."

Brad Jersak, Faculty of NT and Patristics,
Westminster Theological Centre (UK)

—

Walking with Grandfather

A Skeptic's Journey to Spirituality

Michael Hardin

Foreword by Brian Zahnd

Walking with Grandfather: A Skeptic's Journey to Spirituality

Published in the United States of America by
JDL Press
Lancaster, PA 17602

ISBN 978-1500715656

Cover design and interior layout by Lorri Hardin

This Book is Dedicated to:

Edwin A. and Pat Hallsten

Tom Brown Jr. & Lovers of the Earth
Everywhere

Friends of Bill W.

Also By Michael Hardin

The Jesus Driven Life:
Reconnecting Humanity with Jesus

What the Facebook?:
Posts from the Edge of Christendom

Stricken by God?
Nonviolent Identification and the Victory of Christ
Edited by Brad Jersak and Michael Hardin

Peace Be With You:
Christ's Benediction Amid Violent Empires
Edited by Sharon Baker and Michael Hardin

Compassionate Eschatology
Edited by Michael Hardin and Ted Grimsrud

Table of Contents

Foreword
By Brian Zahnd

A generation ago Karl Rahner famously predicted that "the devout Christian of the future will either be a mystic or he will cease to be anything at all." In making this observation the great Catholic theologian was keenly prescient. Indeed, the hope for a vibrant Christianity in the West lies, in part, in a recovery of mysticism. The tyranny of empiricism so characteristic of modernity is at last coming to an end. A Christianity that has no room for the mystics can expect to be increasingly ignored, left to molder in its own arrogant assumptions. The rise of global Pentecostalism in the 20th century is just one harbinger of the type of spirituality that is capable of addressing the spiritual hunger of the postmodern world. Of course there was a time when mysticism was not tangential to Christianity but an integral aspect of Christian experience. After all, we Christians claim it is possible to communicate with God, that miracles are credible, and that the rightful ruler of our planet is a man who was raised from the dead after being crucified two thousand years ago. Mysticism is no outlier to orthodox Christianity.

This why the story Michael Hardin tells in Walking with Grandfather is so timely and is bound to find many eager readers. On the other hand, the account of Michael's spiritual journey—or as he describes it, A Skeptic's Journey to Spirituality—is bound to make some readers cock their heads at its apparent strangeness. But I would suggest that the apparent strangeness has more to do with our residual loyalty to Western empiricism than anything else. As a serious scholar of Karl Barth, Martin Luther, and John Calvin, the author is thoroughly grounded in the Reformed theological tradition of the West. This tradition is intellectually robust (as anyone who has ever spent any time with Barth's Church Dogmatics well knows!) But as Michael Hardin sought healing for his own soul he needed more than academic theology (as valid as this is). What Michael discovered was an ancient path that might be described as aboriginal spirituality. From the point of view of a Christian theologian, aboriginal spirituality is not heterodox, but simply a spirituality rooted in something other than the European Enlightenment—a spirituality not of the ivory tower, but of the moss covered forest.

Today we lament that Christianity arrived in the "new" world as a stowaway in the company of gold crazed Spanish conquistadors and English pilgrims driven mad by the lie of Manifest Destiny. What if there had been a genuine exchange of ideas, a gracious cultural cross-pollination? How much richer might Western spirituality be today if this had occurred? Or do we still cling to the lie of a European spiritual hegemony? Yes, because of a twist of geographical fate, Europeans had the gospel of Jesus Christ and access to the Hebrew and Christian Scriptures. But by the time Columbus made his blundering "discovery," Europeans had already lost much of their aboriginal wisdom—which is to say; they had forgotten that humans belong to the earth. Europeans had learned how to dominate nature, but not how to live with nature. Half a millennium of that trajectory has left our planet in peril. Perhaps, while there is still time, we should become humble enough to consult the wisdom of those who knew how to live in respectful relationship with the rest of God's creation. This was the instinct of Saint Francis of Assisi, a spiritual savant who spoke of brother sun and sister moon, brother fire and sister water. It's this type of integrated spirituality — Christian theology and aboriginal wisdom — that

Michael Hardin explores in his fascinating spiritual travelogue.

With Western culture exhibiting so clearly the symptoms of a deep spiritual malaise, a poverty of soul that is harming both people and planet, we need to bring an end to European hubris. Maybe with chastened humility we can ask if cultures who have lived in close harmony with creation for thousands of years can teach us how to become custodians instead of conquistadors, participants instead of plunderers. For in plundering the planet we have pillaged our souls, leaving us with an emptiness that systematic theology alone cannot fill. So mysticism beckons. We have our Scriptures, we have our Creeds. On these we can rely. But can we also learn to listen to the wise grandfathers and grandmothers of aboriginal spirituality who can teach us much that has been forgotten? I hope so because secularism, which appears to be the only other alternative, leads to nothing but a dead end. Either we become mystics, or it won't be long before we are nothing at all.

Brian Zahnd, Pastor of Word of Life Church and author of *Beauty Will Save the World* and *A Farewell To Mars*

Preface

Usually when I write a book or an essay I try to publish it as soon as possible. In the case of this book though, I didn't. I sat on it for two years. Until now, it just didn't feel like the right time to publish. Why? As I have reflected on this question many answers have come to mind but none more compelling than this: it is difficult to explain how, as a professional theologian, I became enchanted with the natural world and how what I could not find in theology I found through learning from one of the most remarkable teachers I have ever met, Tom Brown Jr. and his mentor Grandfather (Stalking Wolf). Later in the book I will suggest reading recommendations and give you information should you also wish to take classes from The Tracker School and head down this bunny trail into the rabbit hole of mystery, wonder and enchantment.

This then is my story. I have held nothing back; I am revealed here warts, flaws and all. Vulnerability is not easy, for it requires brutal honesty. In the long run, however, knowing oneself truly opens one up to the world and to God. My story begins in my childhood (and whose doesn't) and it wasn't a particularly pretty one although I do have many fond memories of time spent with my father (and yes, even my mother), my brother and sisters, and my best friends Chris and Barry. We all end up playing out the scripts we are given as little children. I reveal some of the scripts that were given to me in this book and how discovering the natural world in all of its splendor, majesty, beauty and wonder helped me to learn new scripts.

This book was written in a span of five days in January 2013. It literally poured out of me. When it was finished, I sat back and took stock of what I had written and felt that for the first time, I could see my life, its direction and trajectory. Since that time, as I have read the manuscript I have come to reflect on this or that episode, event or adventure, sometimes with tears but more often with a wry smile. I made it this far. It's a miracle!

I do want to mention one turning point that is not discussed in this book. In 2005 I read Mark Wallace's *Finding God in the Singing River*. It is one of the few books on theology I read with tears in my eyes for Wallace was describing what I was experiencing. It just so happens that at the same time I was listening to some bird language audio tapes by Jon Young (Wilderness Awareness) and all of the pieces starting coming into place for me.

The year previous to that I had sought to bring my new emerging experience with nature together with my two theological mentors, Karl Barth and René Girard. This exploration was totally new territory for me, fraught with pitfalls and dangers but also bounded with vistas and scenic views that astonished me beyond belief. I have included the essay I wrote at that time at the end of my story. Originally presented as an 'academic' paper to the Colloquium on Violence and Religion (COV&R) in 2004 at Ghost Ranch in New Mexico, it bears all the marks of one struggling to make connections. Like the man who "saw men as trees walking", I too was having my eyes opened. More frightening though was the fact that when I gave this presentation there, in the front row, sat two men who have been father figures to me: René Girard and Robert Hamerton-Kelly; giants among other intellectuals and here was little old me talking about tree hugging at a conference on mimetic theory.

Imagine my surprise when after it was over, René and Bob came to me, effusive in their praise. I was taken totally by surprise. The fact is that they were truly intrigued by the way I had spoken about positive mimesis and what it might mean for ecology. I couldn't have been more delighted when in 2012 Mark Wallace was invited to speak on ecology, mimesis and spirituality at the COV&R meeting in Iowa. His presentation can be found in the journal *Contagion*, Vol. 21. If both theology and ecology are important to you I urge you to read his book *Finding God in the Singing River*.

Thanks to the work of René Girard I had discovered so much regarding our human condition, our negative desire to imitate and create rivals and our twisted interpretations of texts and traditions. I had already had a path set before me in reading Karl Barth for forty years. Still, there was a missing piece and that is what this story is about, finding that one thing that brought it all together for me. This is my story. I wouldn't want you think that you need to take the same journey. I don't need to be imitated to be validated. On the other hand, I hope you find some inspiration to discover your place in God's beautiful, beneficent creation.

As always I am grateful to Lorri for her constant inspiration and for being my partner both in life and on this spiritual journey. I also wish to thank all those who have been my 'partners' in various Tracker classes. Many thanks as well to Mark Ballard who edited the manuscript for me. Finally, thanks to Tom Brown Jr. for opening doors, windows and pathways to a beautiful life.

15

This book is dedicated to my 'father and mother' in the faith, Edwin A. and Pat Hallsten. I am so grateful for their constant faith in me, their love, encouragement and support. From the bottom of our hearts, Lorri and I will always love you!

Peace always.
Michael Hardin, August 2014

Chapter 1
The Worst Week of My Life

I was dragged into it kicking and screaming. I wanted nothing to do with it. That was over a decade ago. Some twelve years later I can say my life has been changed, transformed by having taken a road less traveled. This is the story of how learning to walk the path of a Native American shaman taught me more about Jesus than I could ever have realized.

I was born and raised in the San Francisco Bay Area by a good Roman Catholic father and a mother who struggled with many challenges and difficulties. Her father, my grandfather, was an alcoholic and a pedophile. The family kept his pedophilia a secret although in later years I was made aware of it. My mother had an abusive aspect to her personality and a profound disjunction between what she sought to teach us kids regarding values, and her behavior. I can recall her justification for authority was, "If I say the sky is purple, it is purple because I said so."

Little wonder then that at age 18 I took so quickly to Christian Fundamentalism. The logic was the same. "God said it, I believe it, that settles it for me." However, just as I rebelled against my mother's dysfunctional authority and partook of the early 70's hippie movement, and grew my hair to her chagrin, so within two years, I also began to question the authority of Fundamentalism. My Thompson Chain Reference Scofield Bible no longer felt like it had all the answers.

I had been attending a small Bible College that was supposed to be Conservative Evangelical but for 1976 it really wasn't. We read Kierkegaard, studied gospel criticism and read far more broadly than we were supposed to read. It was a time of great discovery and intellectual turmoil for I saw my Fundamentalist faith developing cracks that could not be plastered over with cheap apologetics. Thus began what is now a theological journey of thirty-seven years.

When I entered seminary at the ripe age of 25 with three small daughters, I had become a convinced follower of the Swiss theologian Karl Barth and secondly of the German theologian Dietrich Bonhoeffer. I had a small growing library filled with Calvin, Luther, the early church fathers and was certain that The Truth could be found by being faithful to that stream. Without knowing it, I lived in my head. Only later would I discover that human beings also have feelings.

Feelings were not allowed in my home growing up. I felt whatever my mother felt or told me to feel. My memory of childhood feelings reads like a bad litany: guilt, shame, fear, an inability to be perfect. Regular corporal punishment was the norm, getting "smacked" across the face an almost daily routine. My refuge lay in books. I hid in between the covers of Madeline L'Engle at 8, J.R.R. Tolkien at 10 and my Encyclopedia Britannica at 12 (a gift from my fourth grade teacher, Mrs. Ashley).

Little wonder then, as an adult, I have taken comfort in books. To this day I cannot for the life of me understand why anyone would want to replace the tactile feel of a book for a device like Kindle.

18

One of my favorite smells is a used book store. There is something life-giving about the musty odor, the creaky wooden floorboards, the books with a memory of many hands before having turned page after page. I am a bibliophile. This is just one of my addictions.

Having graduated seminary I went on to become a pastor. Not a very good one inasmuch as I was doing ministry completely out of my head. Eventually I failed miserably, traveling to the bottom of my personal abyss. I turned to drinking and drugs and had a torrid affair and blew my ministry out of the water with enough emotional C-4 to take out a small town. I wrecked my marriage and ruined my young daughters' lives (not to mention the lives of others involved). I became even more emotionally unavailable, if that was possible.

My redemption came in stages. First, was my wife Lorri. Within months of my collapse she came to me to be reconciled. I clung to her like a drowning man clings to a life buoy on a raging ocean. For the next six years she would love me back to a semblance of spiritual health. Second, in 2000, I met an Episcopal priest, Fr. Jeff Krantz who graciously took me under his wing and saw potential in me that I had long given up on and nurtured my love for theology back from smoldering ashes to a small but glowing fire.

In 1994, the year of The Collapse, I had packed up my books in boxes and stored them in the attic. I spent a lot of time crying by myself, to myself, lamenting the awful way I had destroyed so completely myself and those I loved. Life was a big fog for a long time. Drinking became a way of coping, a daily routine. My idea of a good time was to go to the mall, down six to eight vodka gimlets and go watch a movie that I would not recall. Life had become hell, a hell of my own construction. Yet through it all, there were times I would sit in the attic among my boxed books, smoke a joint and pray. Would God ever use me again? Had I forfeited my calling beyond repair? Had I become a useless blight? Day after day and night after night for years these questions haunted me.

By the turn of the millennium I felt little hope. The next two years between Jeff and Lorri all that would change. Lorri took out a restraining order so I could no longer come home drunk. Jeff insisted on helping me recover my faith and my calling. Little by little I began to see small changes in my life. Little by little there were small glimmers of hope. I was still lost in the woods, but it was as if I could see flashlights way off in the distance searching for me, and once in a while could hear my name called on the whispering wind.

I thought that theology would save me. I had thought, ever since becoming a Fundamentalist that if I just thought the right things in the right way I could make my life better. I began reading in earnest again, now having to catch up on almost eight years of theological trends that had passed me by and left me in the dust. There were so much new material, so many new authors and new trajectories to follow. I felt hamstrung as if I was a crippled horse leaving the starting gate at the Belmont races.

Then came 2002. Little did I know that the year would bring two profound and life-changing events. This is where my new story really began. Looking back I can see the gracious hand of God although at the time it was all but invisible to me. Søren Kierkegaard said, "Life is lived forward, but it is only understood backwards." There is real wisdom in that.

I think it was in January that our middle daughter Arwen came for a visit. She and her mother have always had a close relationship so it was no surprise that when Arwen recommended some books for Lorri to read that they would be read. Although Lorri enjoys reading I don't have a vivid memory of her sitting day after day, week after week reading as she did at that time. She was absorbed. Sometime in March, Lorri began trying to have conversations with me about the books and the author she was reading.

"Michael," she said, "Would you please read one of these books so we can discuss it?" I looked at several of them, "A new journey in spiritual awareness." "One man's journey to nature." "The new Castaneda" (who the hell was that?) Some fool had spent time with an Indian, learned about nature and I was supposed to get excited about this? This was drivel as far as I was concerned. I recall telling Lorri, "I don't have time for this new age bullshit." And that should have been the end of our conversation. Then April happened.

Our daughter came for another visit. She and her mother grew all animated when they were together discussing this new age mumbo jumbo I was sure was worth no more than a plugged nickel. I failed to see how Lorri had gotten suckered into all of this. She is a bright woman. Yet here she was talking all about

---

trees and birds and some mystical nonsense that reminded me of LSD trips I had when I was younger. My irritation slowly grew. A few days into Arwen's visit we decided to take the Long Island Railroad into Manhattan to a Japanese restaurant on 72nd just down the block from the Dakota Building where John Lennon had lived. Some kind of an all you can eat affair for a great price. I hate sushi but if they had Undo noodles and chicken teriyaki I could make a day of it I supposed. So off we went. The visit into the city was nice; the sun was shining and the weather quite cooperative. As we arrived at the restaurant though, it was dark. The sign said it would not be open until 5 pm for dinner. Not to be deterred, Arwen and Lorri decided to take a nice little nature walk through Central Park. How utterly boring!

I took off my backpack to retrieve my book. I always carry a book with me. If I go to the bank or the grocery story I have a book in case I have to wait in line. I am never without a book. Even now there are two theological books in my backpack. Somehow that day my backpack had eaten my book. It was empty! Panic ensued. I looked at Lorri and told her I would head down to 59th street to find a bookstore and get a book and meet her and Arwen back at the restaurant at 5 pm. There are turning points in a person's life that can neither be seen nor measured. They come suddenly, completely unexpected. This was one. Quick as a flash Arwen whipped a book out of her backpack. I could not believe it. It was one of those god-awful new age bullshit books by that crazy nature guy. I know I rolled my eyes so far in the back of my head I could see my occipital lobe. Lorri's argument clinched it, "We really don't have the money for

22

you to go buy another book today, why don't you just read this one?"

I'm not a glutton for punishment (at least not anymore), so I swallowed what was certain to be a sarcastic response and took the book. We'd soon crossed over to Central Park and passed the Strawberry Fields Memorial (John was always my favorite Beatle) and while Lorri and Arwen began walking I opened it. Holding the book at shoulder height so I could see them just over the top of it, I began reading while following them down the paths of the park. At some point before we left the park to head to the Japanese restaurant I had finished it. To say I had been hooked would be an understatement. To say I had been sucked into a vortex would be more like it. For two hours I had read the story of Grandfather, Stalking Wolf. I had never read anything quite like it. I wanted more. No, it was worse than that, I needed more. I had no interest in dinner really; I just needed to keep reading. By the grace of the Librarian in the Sky, Arwen had another book by the crazy nature guy in her backpack that would keep me occupied through my chicken teriyaki and the train ride home and all the next day.

I had entered another world. The only comparable experience that I could recall that was similar was when I discovered Middle Earth at age 10. For weeks I lived and breathed as a hobbit and cried when at the end Sam Gamgee returned home to Rosie. I wanted to read them again as if for the first time. Just to give you an idea of how much Tolkien has affected me, my daughters are Galadriel, Arwen and Melian, my granddaughters are Quelebrian and Laurelin and we have had dogs named Nenya (the ring that

Gandalf wears) and Pippin. This past year Lorri and I visited the Shire set in Mata Mata, New Zealand and other Lord of the Rings and Hobbit sets. Back on that April day, just as I had fallen in love with Middle Earth and its inhabitants and stories so now, even though I can't say I was in love with Grandfather's story, the intrigue I felt was palpable.

I wish I could tell you that this is the end of the story and that you should go out and read the books by Tom Brown Jr. describing his experience of being trained in the ancient ways by Grandfather. It would be just the beginning. A few weeks later Lorri informed me that this Tom Brown fellow had a school located just four hours away in New Jersey. As far as I was concerned the only good thing about Jersey was the fact that it was home to my beloved football team the New York Giants. The only other thing I knew about New Jersey was that it was a toxic waste dump. How was one supposed to learn about nature in the midst of chemicals, pollution and waste dumps?

I knew this wasn't going to be easy. I had been a Cub Scout and for a few years attended Boy Scouts but I hated camping. Something about bugs and heat and cold and bad food I guess. Plus you sweat when you are camping in the summertime. A person would most likely be declared clinically bonkers to want to go camping in the summertime in New Jersey. Lorri was bound and determined to attend the required first class, the Standard Class with or without me. There was no way I was going to lose her to some weird cult or to have some other guys picking up on her, so with great bravado in my voice and trembling in my heart I told her I too was going to do this. She went online to order us two sleeping bags and a three person tent. A few weeks later they arrived and in August we were off to The Farm for the Standard Class. It would become the worst and longest week of my life.

We arrived on a hot and humid Sunday afternoon where we pitched our three person tent with all kinds of other tents around us. No privacy. How was I supposed to have sex with everybody else so close? It was not fair. We unrolled our two sleeping bags and tried to get them inside the tent. They barely fit. With our backpacks and suitcases stuffed around them there was hardly enough room for us to get in to sleep. I then realized it was a three person tent, for pygmies! It was so small that I could not lie straight. Worse was that the only opening was a small mesh screen at the top. It would become an oven. After twenty minutes in it I was ready to be turned over and basted. I slept that night covered in sweat and swearing up a storm under my breath. I was completely and utterly miserable and made sure Lorri knew it. I have heard that misery loves company and I made sure I had all the company I needed.

Breakfast the next morning, Monday, was some gross concoction of gruel, dead bugs, and other disgusting looking things (it was actually some form of seven grain hot cereal but I had never seen the likes of it). It was supposed to be good for you. Could it really be better than eggs and sausage? No way was I having anything to do with it. The class began at 9:00 AM in an old decrepit barn outfitted with wooden benches with no backs. Dust and flies were everywhere. Some fool was outside the barn door tanning a deerskin which drew more flies. The mosquitoes figured they too should join the convention. I was sweaty and now getting filthy. I know that some people's Bibles read that "God made the heavens and the earth." But if God had something to do with the written word and books I figured God preferred to hang out in libraries and bookstores. Nature made no sense. It was chaotic at best. Dirt was bad, and sweat was gross. As a civilized human being I appreciated hot showers, decent food, a comfortable bed and of course, a good book. Sitting in this barn seemed counter-intuitive or immoral.

I don't recall what was served for lunch that day. My memory has done me the favor of forgetting that detail. Probably some sort of road kill and rice. The afternoon class was worse than the morning class. Something to do with building shelters from sticks and leaves. The temperature decided to challenge the top of the thermometer. The flies came from miles around to see what was happening with the deerskin. Along with the slight cooling of dusk the mosquitoes put out a call for their relatives to join them. Spiders decided to make an appearance. Bats flew through the barn rafters at dusk. The toilets were some sort of open air outdoor thing. I figured I could hold it in for three days max, but what would I do come Thursday morning? My misery turned to despair. My despair turned to hopelessness. I now knew I was paying the price for my sins in some circle of Hell. Then it got worse. Dinner was served.

After ten years of attending classes I can still say I don't eat much of it when it is occasionally offered. On that first night, however, I may as well as have been served Klingon intestines. It was called Tracker Stew. Mostly vegetables (which I hate), and some sort of "mystery meat." I could just not bring myself to smell it let alone eat it without triggering my gag reflex. What was worse was watching my wife and the rest of the eighty or so students eat this stuff up like it was Maryland cream of crab soup and then ask for seconds! I knew I had entered the land of fruitcakes then. I recall little about that evening except that it did not cool down at all. I desperately needed a shower. Lack of sleep from the night before had taken my mood into some emotional mosh pit of anger and frustration. Night came. Back we went into the three pygmy tent. Another night of hot misery only this time Lorri had had it with my bitching and moaning and told me so. On Sunday night we had been told that if, on Tuesday morning, we wanted to go home, the school would refund our money. I made it clear to Lorri that I was headed home and I wanted her to come with me. No way. She was as determined to stay as I was to leave.

Tuesday morning came way too early. I had another fitful night of sleep mixed with sweat, despair and anger but was ready to leave. After breakfast of more of the same (which they insisted on serving all week for some strange reason), class began. One of the instructors came up and said "If you would like to go home please raise your hand now." So I waited. I knew there must be at least thirty people who were as miserable as I was. Tick-tock. The seconds passed and no one was raising their hands. Had they all fallen under some magic spell? Could it be that they really liked to eat dead dog for breakfast, lunch and dinner? Now I had my pride to consider. Would I be the only quitter? No way was that going to happen. It was time to put up or shut up.

Tuesday and Wednesday went by in an exhausted dusty blur. I had made friends with a hunter from Michigan named Tom who

---

27

took pity on me. On Thursday we broke the rules and he took me to Burger King for lunch. Never has a cheeseburger and fries tasted so great. I may just as well have been dining in Le Burger du Roi, the famous French fast food restaurant. I ate that burger so slowly savoring every delicious drop of meat, fat and ketchup, chewing ever so slowly as though it was the last meal of a condemned man. I will never forget the grace that hunter Tom showed me that day. It allowed me to endure the rest of the week.

Still, things got worse. On Saturday, the day we were finally allowed by the warden to head to our homes for real food, real toilets, real beds and real showers, the Instructors spoke about the different programs that the school offered. I saw Lorri's eyes light up and knew she was determined to take more classes. The question was what would I do? We discussed it and came up with a plan. She would take the Philosophy track and I would take the Scout track. I will tell you more about the ancient Apache scouts in a later chapter. For now, though, I had to pick something. Being the big, brave, macho type has never been my style, I would not make it in Mark Driscoll's church where I would have to "man up." Why, then, I chose this track is beyond me. But then, little did I know how the gracious hand of Providence was guiding me or that *that* Hand had a twisted sense of humor.

Chapter 2

Macho Is Just Another Word for Stupid

As a child, I loved attending Mass. The stained glass windows, the icons and statues, the smells and bells all contributed to my awe and wonder. I can still recall being given my first Missal, reciting the answers to the catechism for my first Holy Communion and attending CCD (Christian education classes). My first love was a nun. She was young, gentle, caring and beautiful (underneath all those weird clothes). She also happened to wear sandals. That is when I began wearing sandals (take note mimetic theorists!) and to this day still wear them.

I became 'born again' at age 18 and immediately enrolled in Bible College. I have had a thirst for the Bible for as long as I can remember. I have always considered studying theology and Bible to be the most important things I can do. At age 55 I am finally working on my doctorate in theology. I figure that I have read close to 10,000 books on Bible and theology over the past thirty-seven years. I have published five books, so far, to add to others' pain and debt. My home is wall-to-wall bookshelves.

My love affair with the Christian faith is both broad and deep. This goes some way to explaining why I was so uncomfortable with this new age nonsense Lorri was reading in 2002. I just could not understand how she expected me, a trained theologian and critical thinker, to approve of sleight-of-hand mystical spooky spiritual stuff from a non-Christian perspective. After all I had spent my life exploring every path and rabbit trail I could follow where one question led to two more questions and each of those led on further to other questions. I relished discovering answers and exploring the terrain of theology. How could any landscape of nature hope to compete with that?

After we returned from the Standard Class in August I knew I had to sign up for the next course, the Advanced Standard. It was being offered in October, in the New Jersey Pine Barrens where Tom Brown had been mentored by Grandfather. Lorri followed the Standard class almost immediately with the first Philosophy class. She came home quite excited about what she had learned but had no way to communicate with me what had transpired. It is not that she didn't share with me, but I wasn't ready to hear. There is a certain wisdom in the saying 'Let those with ears to hear, listen!"

October came and I dutifully packed up my stuff and the three person pygmy tent which I would now have to myself and was dropped off at the Pine Barrens class site. It was cold that week. Later I would discover it was one of the coldest on record for New Jersey. The temperature hovered around freezing and it rained on and off all week. At least there were portable toilets called "Bobs" because they were from some company with Bob's name painted on the side. You only had to watch out for the black widow spiders that liked to sit and play gin rummy underneath the seat. I found a spot to pitch the pygmy tent and got my gear and sleeping bag inside and headed down for the Sunday night lecture.

Standard Class is a crash course in survival skills. You learn the four most important things about survival: shelter, fire, water, food. You learn how to make a bow drill and a hand drill, how to build a shelter from forest debris, a little about wild edibles and cooking, finding, filtering and purifying water as well as tracking, how to gut an animal and tan its hide and more gross stuff.

Advanced Standard is just what it claims: each of these skills is taken to another level. Here we spent time learning how to make bows and arrows, making and setting traps, basket weaving, how to flint knap our own arrowheads, creating light sources, throw sticks, various stalking steps and other assorted useful skills for people who liked this stuff. That week we were to make our own debris hut. Using a long branch set against a tree and covered with leaves three feet deep we were to sleep in it to stay comfy and cozy. The problem was that eighty students on a small landscape and not enough debris and leaves. I think I managed to get about a foot of leaves on my debris hut. It looked sound enough, surely three feet deep was a bit of overkill. On Tuesday the unthinkable happened. As I went to bed that night, the thermometer registered just above freezing. There are two very difficult things every camper does, undressing to get into a cold sleeping bag at night and getting out of a warm sleeping bag in the morning to put on frigid clothing. That night as I zipped myself in the zipper broke. The gods were not smiling on me. They were laughing at me. I spent the night alternating between frigid and frozen. Thankfully Billy, one of our instructors, lent me a wool blanket for the remaining nights so I was only semi-frozen. The on and off rain meant that it was near impossible to stay dry and the camp fires became my favorite haunt. I would have to say that although my baskets and bowls and spoons, arrows and traps were not works of art, still I had a certain pride that these were actually items I made and could make again if I had to. So even through the cold and rain I managed a certain satisfaction that eluded me during the Standard class. Then came Friday night when we were supposed to sleep in our debris hut.

I took the bowl I had made, put a few small coals from the fire in it, and spread some green pine needles over the coals so they smoldered and smoked and carefully placed it inside my debris hut. This was supposed to drive out all of the spiders and bugs that had decided to use my hut as a squat. With the nimbleness of an Olympic gymnast I made my way into it feet first so as not to bring the entire thing down upon my head. The leaves I had piled on the ground for my ground cover were cold but that was supposed to remedy itself shortly. The problem was that I could see some spiders also still dwelling there with me. That creeped me out. I lay there waiting for my body heat to warm my little shelter. I waited some more. It began raining. Soon my hut was leaking. I waited some more. It just stayed cold. I realized then that three feet of debris was not overkill and all I had managed to do was create an outdoor meat locker. The spiders didn't seem to mind. Sometime around 1 a.m. I made my way, sodden, cold and tired back to my tent and my broken sleeping bag.

I couldn't stand anymore. Thankfully class would end the next day and I could go home. I had pretty much determined that this was the last class I would take. I would gladly leave nature to the hunters and tree-huggers. It just wasn't my cup of tea. Tom said that we were to learn to live luxuriously in nature, in harmony with it, but I knew nature didn't like me very much and I sure didn't like her very much either. I had tried to be really macho but ended up just humiliating myself. I was not as strong as I thought.

In October and November Lorri went on to take three more Philosophy classes, Philosophy 2-4. I missed her terribly when she was gone but after each class she would return with a glow I had not seen on her face since we were dating. I knew then there had to be another man despite all her assurances and protestations. She seemed happier and livelier than she had been in years. I could not figure it out.

It was her return from Philosophy 4 that really ticked me off. She came in the door with a smile as wide as the Grand Canyon. I know there was some small talk and hugs and stuff, she put her things away and showered and we had dinner. Then she said to me "Honey, I finally understand Jesus." Let me get this straight. She has been a church going girl since she was eight years old, always there if the church doors were open, she was a leader in her youth group, she married a pastor and a wanna be theologian. What could she possibly mean? I made some comment that I had spent almost twenty-five years studying the gospels, engaging in all sorts of critical techniques, had learned several ancient languages, studied ancient cultures and I still didn't get Jesus. I mean after all, what was the point of all my hard work if she could just go waltzing off to the woods and let the trees and flowers tell her about Jesus. I was certain then that she had drunk the Kool-Aid except for the fact that she was deadly serious.

She shared with me that in the Philosophy classes they had learned how to do things that I knew were well nigh impossible. How to heal or live in the spirit world. I half expected her to say she could turn lead into gold. The skeptic in me was on full alert. But what she said next floored me. She said, "In church I was taught that Jesus could do miracles because he was divine, he was God. What we learned in Philosophy class was that doing the miraculous is every person's birthright, it is just a matter of listening to the Creator." I wondered about this. Let me see if I got this straight. I had spent decades reading books about Jesus and his culture, incurred an obscene amount of debt to graduate seminary and all she had to do was go hug a few trees to understand Jesus? It just wasn't right!

I had no idea what she was talking about. She shared with me the meditation she had learned to use. I just could not get it. It seemed about as useful as mold on bread. I figured she had either been brainwashed or had learned another language. Either way I was done with this nonsense. All I had managed to do was learn about heat, cold, sweat, dirt, rain, and biting wind.

The winter of 2003 I tried to get excited about my next class which wouldn't be until spring, May to be exact. I made the mistake of sharing with some of my friends at work about what I had learned in class and was nicknamed 'Dancing with Squirrels.' Fat lot of good any of this stuff did me. As spring approached and the weather became warmer, Lorri and I began to take walks in Alley Pond Park in Queens not far from where we lived on Long Island. I tried to pay attention to things like plant identification or animal tracks. But I had not practiced what I had learned so, of course, that was a disaster. Still, I did enjoy the trails and walks we took.

—

The month of May came to the East Coast that year in all her beauty. I recall the temperature was moderate and the flowers gorgeously arrayed in brilliant colors swaying in the perfect breezes. It was time once again to pack up the three pygmy tent and camping gear to head back to the Pine Barrens. This would be the Advanced Tracking and Awareness class. I had no idea what was in store. I have since learned that it is useless to try and guess what any class will teach me. Expectations are not helpful. Lorri dropped me off in late May, a week before my forty-sixth birthday. Even though I had determined not to take any more classes I still wanted more than anything to take the Scout class. I had heard so much about it. The class I was about to take was the final prerequisite to the Scout class which would be offered three weeks later in June. Little did I know that the beginning of my transformation lay just days away.

Chapter 3
What's That Smell?

In the period I now refer to as my healing time, from 1994-2001, I could not afford a therapist. Shortly after my collapse in the late summer of '94 when Lorri and I had moved back in together I went to a local Catholic church to see if there might be priest from whom I could receive spiritual guidance. Other than pastoring a congregation I had no skills except for waiting tables and any given shift did not mean great money. Rent, utilities, food, meant that every penny was necessary to get by. When the day of my appointment came to visit the local priest who did spiritual counseling work came I went in and told him the whole sad and sordid tale of my decline and fall. I was overjoyed when he said that he could help me and was willing to take me on as a client. He then said it would be $50 a session. $50! I walked away sadly in need of such help but unable to afford it.

So it came about that I turned to the only therapy I knew, I picked up my guitar and began playing until at some point in the pain a song would emerge. I wrote over a hundred songs in those years, I kept around sixty-five of them. One of them begins:

> "There are times that call for changes
> in every person's life.
> There are times when we need to let go of our greed
> make better what is right."

Even though this song was written in 1995, it wasn't until May of 2003 that I would find out just what it meant to really undergo transformation. For most of life I've been a firm believer that change is not good. It certainly isn't fun. Take puberty. One moment one is a happy go lucky innocent child, full of imagination and the next moment one is an acne-covered, insecure, sexually-obsessed teenager. Change isn't all it is cracked up to be. I much prefer stasis, things just staying the same. I was about to be proven wrong about myself and about change.

The Advanced Tracking and Awareness class is as described. One learns more about tracking and awareness. In order to really understand this you must realize that the Apache had developed a system of examining tracks and observing a possible 4,500 different things one could see in a track. I had assumed from my previous classes that tracking was primarily about track identification. That's a deer track, that's fox track, that sort of thing. I thought I knew how to read a track. What I learned is that a track is a window into an animal's or a human's very soul, so to speak. Once can tell an animal's age in a track, its gender, when it last ate or defecated, which direction its head is turned, what it was looking at when the track was made, whether there is disease and where, what its mood was and how fast or slow it was moving at the time. That's only the beginning.

Tom is one of the world's, if not the world's, foremost tracker. He can track anything on any surface. Just to give you an idea of how good Tom is let me tell you a story. I don't recall which class it was but Tom drove in one morning early to have his

—

coffee and meet with his instructors before class as he always does. That morning I saw him watching in a crouch while a cricket walked along the sand path. He was tracking a cricket on sand! That was insane. Now you need to know that the Tracker School has a no fraternization policy. This means that people are not supposed to pick up on one another, they are there to learn. So here's Tom following this cricket when it crosses a human footprint which then catches his eye. "Billy!" he yelled to one of the instructors, "Come here." Billy came running over. I was standing five feet away. "Do you see this? There's nothing like a track of sexual satisfaction. I told those volunteers, I told those volunteers not to do it." Then Tom followed those tracks to the poor unwitting volunteer who had found a partner the night before from among the students and chastised him.

We began the week with awareness exercises, learning how to determine the baseline of a given area. In order to do this we would go out each morning, sometimes several times a day to sit in an area for twenty or thirty minutes in a very still quiet meditative state. This gives time for the birds, wildlife and insect life to return to the area in their natural state. One can then listen to the bird language or watch which animals might use a certain trail system or how many ticks can crawl on one's legs at any given moment. At first I found this kind of sitting rather difficult, like being forced to listen to John Cage compositions while eating cauliflower. There was one morning though, when the sun had just risen above the tops of the pine trees and we went to our sit spots. The disturbance I created when coming to my sit spot quickly returned to baseline and in short succession I was visited by a fox, a raccoon and a rabbit. All walked within three feet of my area. I was close to rapture. Except for a zoo, I had never been close to any other animals, and even then that was a petting zoo. I could not believe my good fortune.

My favorite exercise took place that Monday night. We really weren't told what was going to happen but that we had to get in our bathing suits and bring our blindfolds. Were we going swimming at night? The stream was cold, but anything was possible. Just at dusk we were led as a group of 70 or so down the sand road outside the camp and up a trail to a firebreak. We were then lined up on the firebreak about ¼ mile away from where the camp was. All that stood between us and camp was pure dense forest. Blindfolds went on. We were told we would hear a drumbeat off in the distance, once every minute. Our task was to make our way, barefoot, blindfolded and in our swim suits, in the dark to the drum.

At the signal, the line which had been quiet began moving slowly through the thick brush. From the quiet erupted language that would make a seasoned sailor blush. Never had I heard so much swearing, never had I #*&%ing swore so %$#*ing much. Every step on a rock or a broken twig elicited another *$#@&ing curse. It was a miserable %#**%ing beginning. The drum boomed in the distance. However, whereas the drum had just been heard to my left, now it was to my right. I would turn to go in that direction and now it was behind me. I swore that $@^&%ing drummer was moving around me and not staying in one place. Smack! Hit my head on an overhanging branch. This was insane and no fun at all. No fun, that is, until I remembered how I was supposed to conduct myself.

—

I was supposed to Fox Walk which is a very specific type of stalking step that one uses to "feel" the ground before placing one's weight. That way one can discern whether the ground underneath has a twig or branch that could break and make sound or whether the ground is rocky, etc. I quickly slowed and began placing my feet in the manner I was taught. Others around me must have realized the exact same thing because less than two minutes after all 70 of us began moving from the firebreak to the camp there was a virtual silence. I swore I was all alone out there such was the quiet.

I also knew that others were practicing their 'breath to surrender' and listening to their Inner Vision. I stopped, took a deep and slow breath, let it out and surrendered to the earth. I then began to slowly fox walk to the sound of the drum. I don't recall hitting any other branches or walking into any trees, stepping on any rocks or getting scratched by brambles. I had entered a zone where I was a spectator within myself, just letting my mind be quiet and allowing the earth to dictate my body movements. Twenty minutes later I arrived at the drum. I think I was the fourth or fifth student to arrive. The only thing was that it wasn't twenty minutes that had elapsed, as I had thought, but over two hours. Two hours! I could not believe how my sense of time had become so distorted. Yet once I entered the zone of quiet in my fox walk and surrendered self, I had so relaxed that the exercise was a delight.

Lorri and I still use the Night Drum Stalk when we lead retreats. The first time we led one it was amazing to see the exact replication of my experience. How for the first minute or two people are completely out of touch with the earth, yet within a very short time they are moving with ease and grace. Just when you think they are going to walk right into an oak, they pause and shift to the left or right and move past it. Ducking underneath branches is common. It is all so strange for it is night and these folks are blindfolded and have no idea what lies in front of them. Each time we have taught this exercise everyone has had a great experience of learning how to surrender and trust the Inner Voice to guide them.

A few years ago we had an opportunity to invite some African American pastors from New Orleans Ninth Ward to join us following the devastation of Hurricane Katrina in 2005. They had come to attend our Making Peace Conference which is an annual week long event where we combine bible study, native skill work and the application of René Girard's mimetic theory. We were about forty that night as we made our way to the wooded area of the park where we were to participate in the Night Drum Stalk. After I had explained to everyone what they were going to do, I asked them to put on their blindfolds. Surrounded by local Mennonites and pastors from around the country, one of the New Orleans pastors turned to me and whispered, a little ironically, "Michael, do you realize you are asking a black man to go blindfolded into a white man's woods?" Later that night we had quite a laugh about that but I also realized the ways in which a simple exercise could bring such vivid cultural memories to mind.

Awareness is not our natural human condition; it is skill that must be taught. In our post 9/11 world we see the importance of awareness every time we enter an airport or train station. The

TSA is constantly reminding us to be vigilant. Animals have a much keener sense of awareness than humans, they must or they would not survive. Since I have been tuned into living a life of awareness (or at least trying to), I am amazed how many people around me live unaware with their ears stuffed with music, or talking or texting on their cell phones or how they look at the ground when they walk. As Tom puts it, "We are aware of what we chose to be aware."

We had begun that week tracking deer on sand. Not so difficult you might say and you would be right. We then moved to tracking foxes on forest debris and ended the week tracking mice on moss. Our eyes bled, so to speak. Tracking is an art and a science. I cannot say that I have kept up my tracking skills to the level of my hopes or desires but knowing the basics and just remaining aware of them, repeating over and over again what I need to remember has helped me to remain aware when I talk a walk in the woods.

Later that week we also delved into natural camouflage, using ash, charcoal, clay and the forest debris. I have pictures of myself and others in class sitting beside a road in what would be plain view yet it is very difficult to pick us out such was the quality of our camo. The only problem with camo is that it doesn't exactly come off easily, particularly the charcoal.

Tom tells a story of how one time he had a class camo-up and then lie in the brush on either side of the road. He was then going to come down the road to critique each student's camo. Just at that moment a group of bikers came roaring down the sand road that leads into the Primitive Camp. Tom stood in the middle of the road by himself and announced that they would have to leave, and that they were trespassing on private property. One biker huffed, "Yeah? Who's going to make us? You and what army?" Tom yelled, "Class, Stand up!" Suddenly, from out of nowhere, all along that road students emerged, many within feet of the bikers. They could barely control their bikes as they spun on the sand to get the hell out of there.

By far the most exciting experience for me was the Friday night "spirit-tracking" exercise. In groups of four we were led to an area rich in fox tracks on forest debris. The first three tracks were marked by an instructor with a popsicle stick stuck in the ground at the front of each track. Each person in turn would then use whatever light they chose to mark the next four tracks until the following sixteen tracks were marked. Then all lights were turned off and we were to listen to our Inner Voice and place our next popsicle sticks where we sensed the tracks were. I have recorded in my class notes that I got all four of my tracks with light correct and 3 out of 4 of my "spirit tracks" correct. That was when I knew I had passed from one way of life to another. I was beyond ecstatic.

One can take a bucket shower at the Primitive Camp. That week the best I could do was to wash myself in the stream but I was certain I was quite ripe when Lorri was to pick me up on Saturday. A dozen of us and our gear packed into the van for our ride out of the Pine Barrens to our pick-up spot. I noticed several people doing the sniff under the arm test, so I did as well. Not too bad I thought. The weekend before the class Lorri and I had gone camping, where we roasted chicken and marshmallows over the fire. So I knew my last real shower with soap, shampoo and hot water was at least eight days previous, still I determined the odor coming off of me was really not all that offensive.

When Lorri arrived to pick me up to drive four hours back to Long Island, she could not breathe through her nose. She had caught a terrible cold. I felt sorry for her but let it go. We stopped on the way home at a diner we like where I could enjoy some 'real food.' Somewhere in north Jersey before we hit the Outerbridge crossing that would take us to Staten Island and thence to Long Island, I needed to close my eyes for a moment. I must have fallen into a deep sleep for when I awoke the smell in the closed car was so bad I thought I was going to vomit. I immediately rolled down the window to let out the noxious fumes but they would not go away. I vowed then and there to never go a day without a shower. Lorri quipped that if she could smell she was certain I would have walked home. It was horrid, the odor one can only find in pathology labs exponentially magnified. It was the smell of death.

When I got home I was informed that I was to immediately place all clothes directly into the washing machine and then I took a shower and washed and scrubbed myself several times. I was certain that whatever smell was coming from me was gone. Lorri then handed me a spray bottle of cleaner and told me to go scrub the seat in the car where I had sat and any surface I had touched and reminded me once again it was a good thing she had clogged sinuses. I could only think about all those poor people in the diner. I was certain I had ruined many good meals.

—

Lorri needed to go to the store so she brought our five year old granddaughter out to the car and strapped her into her car seat in the rear. Quelebrian immediately began complaining about the horrible smell. Lorri stopped the car, opened the rear door and discovered under the driver's seat some raw chicken that had been festering in the heat for over a week. It was the chicken we had not eaten on our camping venture before class. Well, at least it really wasn't me that stunk up the joint after all!

Although this class had nothing to do with my faith, still it has, upon reflection, informed it. If someone had told me that I would be able to walk in the dark blindfolded without crashing into trees or pick out fox tracks in the dark without seeing I would have told them they were either delusional or wondered if I was on Candid Camera. Neither of these experiences fit inside the box I had created for myself. They forced me to open my intellectual box to at least acknowledge that I had accomplished what I had accomplished. How had I done it? I hadn't figured that out yet, but the fact remained I had done it. Better, I knew that more was to come in the Scout class.

That Saturday when we returned home I went into our little backyard to sit and enjoy the late afternoon and reflect. All of a sudden the small area of our lawn began to shift before my very eyes and, Lo and Behold, I could see a perfect trail of cat tracks up and down by the flower garden bed. I ran in the house, got my popsicle sticks and tagged every one of them. I then took a walk around our neighborhood and it was as if someone had placed little lights everywhere on every lawn: cat tracks, dog tracks, squirrel tracks, and human tracks (I hadn't learned to see bird tracks yet). As dusk settled in and I reveled in the coming night, a visitor came up to me on the back porch. A raccoon just waltzed up to about two feet in front of me, stayed for a few minutes and then turned around and walked away. That had never happened to me before. I took it as a sign. Of what? I didn't know or even care. But whatever it was, it was bound to be good.

Chapter 4

Invisibility

Over the years I have read a number of books that address the relationship between science and religion. Some of them see no connection between the two, suggesting that science and religion are worlds apart. Some see areas where science and religion converge. I am not a scientist and so the nuances of biology and chemistry or the math of physics are beyond me. I often wonder though if those who engage in these debates are willing to recognize that we all have mental boxes we inhabit. Some, one might say many, have very small boxes. That is, their worldviews are set in stone and don't allow for anything to get in or get out. Some minds are like cement, all mixed up and permanently set. Others seem to recognize that they think inside a box but their walls are more porous and so their box is expandable.

When I first began this journey of walking with Grandfather and learning aboriginal survival skills, I found out rather quickly that my intellectual box was as small as my pygmy tent. I had been stuffing it full of more and more of the same thing and cowered at the possibility that life might, in fact, be more wondrous that I had imagined. There is a certain comfort in living in a world of rational security where everything can be explained within the system of the box. I had the right box thankfully and others the wrong boxes. What I was unwilling to see at that time was that I was living in fear. Fear of change, fear of being wrong, and fear that God would no longer like me if I unzipped my 'pygmy tent mind' and ventured outside into the dark forbidding wilderness of life. This fear was deeply rooted. As a child I had great fear of my mother. She could lash out for any reason and Smack! My siblings and I were raised to be perfect little white middle class suburban children who should not bring any shame whatsoever on their parents. When my stepfather first met us he said to my mother, "Shirley, you don't have children, you have robots."

My neighborhood was peppered with bullies. The route I took to school and back each day was an obstacle course of avoiding the houses where the bullies lived. There were at least five, maybe six houses where I would cross the street, back and forth, so as not to cross some imaginary boundary where I would be threatened or have to run for my life. I learned other fears as well, fear of storms, of insects and spiders, of strangers, fear of being caught doing wrong, fear of police. Later I would learn still other fears. My entire existence was one lived in fear, except for books. The world of ideas was not a fearful one. Until I became a born again Fundamentalist, then fear came back with a vengeance. Now there were approved reading lists and the great Satan himself to fear. There was fear of liberalism, immorality and, God forbid, wrong theology which could damn me to an eternal hell.

Fear is *the* single greatest weapon of ignorance and darkness. It stops us from moving forward in life more than anything else. We now live in a world dominated by fear. Fear of economic collapse, fear of terrorism, fear of being shot while at a mall or movie theater, fear of the strange and unknown. The television series Fear Factor says it all. We are being culturally conditioned to live in fear. Yet is it not the case that Scripture says, "perfect love casts out fear? (I John 4:18)" I have often wondered what a world, what *my* world, might look like if I feared nothing, not even death. I was soon to find out. It took place in stages. The first stage was the Scout class.

If you go online you will discover a few things about the Apache scouts. The Wikipedia article, for example, describes them (and I am fairly certain this was written by a student from one of Tom's Scout classes):

> The scouts trained their own clansmen in an intense process that lasted over ten years. Young children within the clan would be closely observed by current scouts and elders. Those who showed promise in skills—such as awareness, tracking and hunting, physical fitness, and selflessness—would be selected to undergo the training process.
>
> Training included advanced techniques of camouflage and invisibility as well as of observation and stalking. These skills led to their nicknames as "shadow people" and "ghosts". The scouts became masters of wilderness survival, excelling beyond the skills of the lay clansmen. This was necessary, for they often had to leave the clan for extended periods of time with nothing but a buckskin loincloth and perhaps a stone knife.

This is perhaps as brief a definition as one might give them. There is an interesting website called apachescout.com that has a home page with just a full moon and no visible way of entry. I guess one must know the secret to getting in. And that makes sense. The Apache scouts were a highly trained, very intelligent medicine society. Their skills were well beyond the ordinary. Far be it from me to violate that code with what I learned in class. Why? The week I spent in the Scout class has turned into a life-long commitment to a way of life that respects all life. However, like Tom Brown has done in his book *The Way of the Scout*, I have had certain experiences that are mine and therefore I feel the freedom to share them.

As I said, I am afraid of bullies. Why? I do not know how to fight or defend myself. Rather I should say I did not know until Scout class and that is where my faith and learning Grandfather's skills met head on like two trucks barreling down the highway from opposite directions. I admire those who practice martial arts and can defend themselves. Most people learn a martial art solely for the purposes of defense. However, there are always rotten apples in the bunch that learn an art form and then use it to pump up their ego. They pick fights just to show off their skills. Like the great martial arts masters, the Apache Scout was a person of peace (for the scouts included both women and men). The Scout was the last to pick up the lance or the knife. They avoided conflict at all costs, seeking other ways to be at peace with all people. War was just not in their blood. Yet, in Scout class we practiced martial skills.

I was torn betwixt and between. Hadn't Jesus said "Love your enemy"? Hadn't Jesus refused to take up arms and engage in violent revolution? Hadn't Jesus laid down his life and offered forgiveness instead of screaming for retribution? Why then was I learning how to handle a knife as a weapon? I struggled with this day after day in that class. What possible good could come for a pacifist like me to learn how to defend myself when the whole point of Christian existence, as I understood it, was about taking up one's cross and laying down one's life? I confess to still struggling with it. It is not my place to judge those who have learned to be warriors, but there is a chasm, an abyss between the way of the Scout and the modern soldier who is taught to "kill, kill, kill" and dehumanize his enemy. This much I know.

As the Wikipedia article notes, scouts learn the art of camouflage. They learn to use the landscape to their advantage. They know how and where to hide. More importantly though is the art of

—

camouflaging one's spirit. What do I mean? Have you ever been in a room full of people when someone walks in and suddenly the mood of the room changes either for better or worse? We can easily enough detect a person's spirit or attitude; it radiates beyond one's self and affects others. So too in the wilderness, we are more than just our physical presence. So we must learn how to camouflage our "hidden" self because it is not really all that hidden. It too can be sensed by animals and others on the land. A scout learns to become invisible on both a physical and a spiritual level.

We had spent the week as teams learning how to stalk and camouflage, and work together in the daylight and the dark. We had been playing "war games" against each other. On Friday night we were to go out and 'scout' the public areas where people would be partying and most likely littering and destroying the landscape. Our task was not to do any harm or injure anyone; rather we were "never to be seen" and to engage in a form of psychological warfare. We might go in and move a cooler or rearrange the chairs of a group, that sort of thing; just enough to be close to them without giving ourselves away. "Never be seen" was our creed.

My team had been excellent all week. We really didn't have a macho alpha male who demanded attention. We had walked trails and moved through the forest and swamp paying close attention to our formation and the use of hand signals. We had learned the art of quick compromise and negotiation when discussing changes to our missions. So when Friday night came we were all a bundle of nerves for now we would have a real "enemy", Mr. and Mrs. John Q. Public.

Now the Pine Barrens of New Jersey have somewhat of a Wild West reputation about them. Locals are known as "Pineys." One might think of them as the hicks or rubes of that part of Jersey. If we had been in the South we might have called them rednecks. Many of them drove big four wheel drive pickups and carried loaded firearms; we had to be very careful.

We left camp shortly after dusk. We had been given our mission area. We were to proceed what felt like a couple of miles to an area that was a huge expanse of sand with islands of pine and low-lying blueberry bushes and some scrub oak. The moon was almost full that night so we could see rather far into the distance which also meant that we could be seen. So we took great care in getting to our designated area. It had rained every day that week so while this night was clear it was also damp, which was good for us for it meant that as we went through an area the ground was less likely to betray our sound. It meant on the other hand that we had to be careful about leaving our own tracks.

As we approached the "sand desert" we could hear the strains of rock music. Someone was partying. As we got closer I could make out the licks of Carlos Santana on the night air. We drew into the brush to make our final plans for our "assault." Our problem was that the area was a patchwork of sand roads all leading different directions dotted by these "small islands" or areas of scattered brush and pine. There was really nowhere to hide on these islands once we got there. How were we supposed to get eight people into an area, conduct a little Psy Ops, and return without being seen? Someone had to go scout out an appropriate place of insertion. That person turned out to be me.

There are several ways to cross a road at night that we had learned imitating animals. I choose the deer walk. If done correctly I would look like a deer crossing the road in the darkness. I crossed the road, trying my best not to leave my footprints in the sand and landed on the party island. My group was back hidden on the other side of the road in dense brush. I was now alone. Guess who came to visit? Mr. Fear. I knew the full moon illuminated me as I lay there in the sand. The music was much louder, I could see the fire that the party had blazing and could count a number of them. It seemed like there were a hundred but in reality there were only ten or twelve. Then I heard voices of two people talking. Worse they were coming towards me. I crawled toward a blueberry bush that was about two feet high and buried my head as deep into it as I could and splayed the rest of my body out in some strange shape. I prayed that my camo was good. The voices began to get closer. Then things went from bad to worse.

I had placed myself on the triangular end of an island where three sand roads intersected. The closest tree was a good twenty feet away. The voices coming toward me on one road could not have been more than sixty feet away and were coming slowly. Then a car engine started up. Back in the party area headlights came on and the car pulled out. It left the party area and headed down the sand road, maybe it was going on a beer run. Wherever it was going as the voices came nearer, the headlights of the car washed over me. Full moon, car headlights and I was going to be seen. I was going to be the one who brought dishonor to my group. I may have to flee for my life.

One of the sayings of Grandfather that has meant so much to me is "The greater the need, the greater the results." I had an intense need at that point. I can't say exactly what happened but somewhere deep inside me a fierce calm took over and I relaxed into my position. I was the sand, the blueberry bush. I was just an old dead log. I could see the two figures pass three feet in front of me. I could see them looking my way. The car turned down another road; the voices passed by me and I slowly and very quietly exhaled. Then the voices came around behind me. I could not turn my head but I could hear them, again no more than three or four feet behind me. They passed on and headed back up the road to the other side of the party island.

I waited a few minutes and slowly got up to a crouch and made my way back to the edge of the road bordering the brush where the rest of my team lay in waiting. The smaller sand roads of the Pine Barrens are about ten to twelve feet across. I didn't do a deer stalk across the road or a raccoon roll. I imitated Greg Louganis and dove across the road crashing into the brush. I am sure I made enough noise to be heard clear to Trenton. I made my way to the group. They were whispering to me in very animated voices having seen the whole thing. I couldn't talk though, my mouth was so dry. I had no spit. My heart was trying to break my ribcage to get out and I needed oxygen, I thought I must have been huffing from a paper bag. One of my mates handed me some water and after a bit we decided that that was enough adventure for the night and headed back to camp.

There is more to the story than I can tell. What I can say is that I don't know why I wasn't seen that night. Had I actually gone invisible? Was my camo that good? I really doubted it. Or perhaps was my need so great that somehow, some way I had managed to enter the sphere of invisibility?

A few years later that was put to the test. Lorri and I had taken more classes by then and so understood the mechanics of being one with the creation much better. As I recall it was a lovely fall day when we took our walk in the Lancaster County Park. It was just a nature walk, the kind of thing people do when they want to get outside and enjoy some fresh air. We were walking a trail that had a valley off to our left. Lorri was about ten feet behind me. We were not camouflaged and I am sure we smelled like soap and Head and Shoulders. All of the sudden a seven point buck bounded up the slope between us. We immediately froze and went into Owl Vision or wide angle vision and "dropped" into invisibility. The normal response of a deer at that time of year would have been to turn and run back down into the brush and trees of the valley. This one stopped. It was confused. It would look one way toward Lorri and past her and then toward and past me. It pawed the ground with its right front hoof and snorted. For close to five minutes the deer tried to see something that was no longer there. It moved a few feet closer and repeated the pawing, head turning and snorting. Then it finally bounded away.

We were thrilled. Something had happened. The deer should just have bolted. We were easily enough seen and could surely be smelled. Yet the confusion in the deer's eyes and its attempt to draw us out indicated to us that we had achieved a level of invisibility. In later classes this became a technique we would practice. As we returned to the car that day I thought of the story of Jesus in his hometown of Nazareth where he preached a sermon that almost got him killed. As the crowd was driving him toward a cliff, the text says that he walked right through them. I cannot say that Jesus became invisible but there were days I wondered how deeply he had gone into learning the skills of a shaman. I was about to find out.

55

Chapter 5
Science and Religion

I really struggled after this to integrate all of this new experience with my theology. I had not yet discovered the work of theologian LeRon Shults which has since given me a framework to put all of these pieces together in a more coherent fashion. At that time, the opportunity, indeed the need, to think through this stuff through in terms of mimetic theory and theology overwhelmed me. Thus it was that I ended up writing the essay *Ecospirituality* which I would present the following summer to the Colloquium on Violence and Religion (which is reproduced at the end of this book). Reading it now, some ten years down the line, I smile because I recall those days vividly as I really struggled to make connections between spirituality, faith and science. It is far from an elegant essay yet somehow I still find reading it instructive, both as to my state of mind at the time and as a foundation for learning to integrate all I have learned from so many different teachers.

We live in a quantum universe. At the subatomic level life or energy is on the move. At that level of physical reality there is a certain ambiguity or what physicist Werner Heisenberg calls "the principle of indeterminacy." To put it very simply, scientists can measure where a particle, like a photon, is, or they can measure its trajectory but they cannot do both at the same time. They have also discovered that the very act of measuring subatomic particles affects the particles. There is no longer such a thing as the detached objective observer. All of our observation affects what it is we are observing.

Our reality is all interconnected. On the physical level one might say we are interconnected with all life, from the stars to oceanic microbes. Everything affects everything else. The poet says, "No one is an island unto himself." Modern science, at least in theoretical physics, no longer works as though the scientist is not part of the actual process of experimentation. Our questions are not neutral, they are theory-laden. This means that the answers we receive are already influenced by the questions we ask.

In the 20th century we have seen a similar shift in psychology and sociology to a relational model. Psychologists no longer treat patients, they treat systems. If a person comes for treatment a good psychologist knows that the patient is part of a larger family system and that it is the system that is dysfunctional, not just the patient. In the same way literary critics and philosophy have hammered away at the concept of the autonomous subject until it no longer exists except in the minds of the uneducated. Similarly, sociologists study groups, not individuals. One way for us to come to terms with all of this interconnectedness might be to recognize that there are no such things as individuals. There is no such thing as a Michael Hardin. I am, or I exist, only in my relationships. I am the fruit of all the relationships I have had in my life. In the word coined by René Girard we might say that if we are no longer to believe that we are individual we might say we are *interdividual*.

This way of understanding ourselves raises all sorts of new questions not the least of which has to do with what we call free will. Most theological debates about free will have been raised in the context of the notion of election. Has God so predetermined all reality that our choices don't matter? Are we just puppets in the some cosmic theater? Advocates of free will have argued that each person is a free moral being capable at a certain age (known as the age of accountability) of making their own choices and being responsible for those choices. Christians were not the first religious or philosophical people to debate these issues. Both the ancient Jews and Greeks also talked about whether life was determined or whether human choice played a role.

I have often wondered if the debates on determinism and free will are really asking the right questions. It seems to me that as long as we conceive of humans as individual rather than *interdividual* we will be asking questions that have no real world answers. If you ask the wrong question you are sure to get the wrong answer. The question of free will becomes especially acute in the light of certain discoveries in the cognitive science of neurophysiology and imitation theory.

In 1996 researchers in Parma, Italy discovered that the neural pathways in our brains had certain types of cells called mirror neurons. These neurons 'fire' every time we move a muscle, turn our head, lift our hand, or take a walk. They were originally thought to be action oriented neural systems. What follows is an apocryphal story that illustrates that discovery. Researchers had a monkey whose head had electrodes attached to it so they could measure which parts of the brain activated for which actions. If a monkey picked up a banana, then certain neural pathways lit up on the computer monitor; if the monkey peeled the banana other pathways lit up and if the monkey ate the banana then other pathways would light up. So far so good.

Then one day a researcher walked by a monkey and spied a banana on the counter. He picked it up. The monkey watched. However, on the computer screens the same neural pathways lit up as if the monkey had actually picked up the banana. The researcher peeled the

---

58

banana. Again the monkey simply observed the behavior but the neural pathways in the monkey's brain lit up as if the monkey had peeled the banana. Finally the researcher took a bite of the banana and the monkey's brain lit up as though it was eating the banana. What the researchers discovered was that the same cells and neural systems fired for both action and perception. Whether we do something, watch someone else do something or imagine ourselves doing something, the same pathways fire in our brains. Think about the implications of this. Our brains cannot determine perception from action. Whether I eat a cheeseburger or watch you eat a cheeseburger, either way my brain uses the same neural system.

This research confirmed an insight developed by Stanford professor René Girard that we imitate one another, not just in action but also in perception. The way he puts it is that we imitate one another's desires. Wants or desires do not spring autonomously from some mysterious place within the self, they are non-consciously imitated. In short, this simple neural and social fact puts to rest any discussion of free-will. We are not free, all of our choices are determined, not by God, but by others. And this is where the debate takes a new turn. It is not God who has determined our lives; it is we ourselves who determine each other's lives by what we desire. By framing this issue of determinism and free-will simply in human terms and not invoking some divine puppet master, we are able to get beyond the impasses that have beset this debate for over 2,500 years.

Why is this important? It is important because I am going to talk about intention and choice. One of the keys to understanding Grandfather's philosophy is to understand the role that intention and choice play. As a theologian I knew that the apostle Paul had addressed the breakdown between intention and choice in his letter to the Roman Christians (chapter 7). One of the reasons many folks do not believe in experiences outside of their own box can be directly traced to the breakdown between intention and choice.

I figured that it was at the intersection of the neurophysiological and the subatomic quantum level that I could most easily reflect on the relation between science and religion. So far, my experiences in the Tracker School classes were easily assimilated to my faith and my rudimentary understanding of certain sciences. Even if I could not understand how I had managed to "spirit track" a fox or how I had become invisible I could put both down to a certain amount of luck or other's people's lack of awareness. I had no explanation for what had happened nor did I need one. That they had occurred there was no doubt, that I needed a rational or logical justification did not feel necessary at that time. I knew that given time I might be able to figure out what had happened.

I have always been a bit of a skeptic; I simply don't believe what I am told. I have a need to prove things to myself even though I wasn't born in Missouri. I now know that my radical rejection of both my mother's arbitrary authority and the authoritarianism of my experiences in conservative Evangelicalism inform this position I have taken. I don't expect anyone to believe anything I say, just because I said it. In fact I hope you don't. I hope there is a little bit of skepticism as you read.

Each class I took came with a healthy dose of skepticism. If, at first, I hated getting dirty and sweaty, later classes would be intellectually and spiritually challenging. After taking the Scout class in the summer of 2003, Lorri took a class on Advanced Awareness from which she has plenty of her own tales to tell. Later that fall I took a class called Expert Tracking. Here we learned the value of building a tracking box in our backyards, and how weather and humidity affected a track's age. We intensified our study of 'pressure releases' in a track. I will never forget tracking squirrels in an area Tom called 'Satan's Carpet.' It was an area of pine trees with a thick layer of pine needles that had accumulated over the years. It was like 3-D tracking because one was looking for the tiniest of claw marks on pine needles. Sometimes a claw mark would be on a top layer, another claw mark from another toe two layers down, and another claw mark a third layer down. It wasn't long before I understood why it had been given such a diabolic name. Our eyes bled (metaphorically). It was hard work, but it taught me to pay attention to the details, something I have also applied when I read biblical texts.

2004 was a turning point year. In all I would end up taking eight week long classes and three weekend workshops. I had worked through enough of my skepticism and was starting to have fun. I realized that dirt and sweat actually came off in a shower. We purchased an honest to goodness three person tent (which we still use today) and two decent sleeping bags (which I found out two weeks ago are not exactly winter-rated). We have an entire bookshelf dedicated to field guides and books on the natural world, natural skills and Native American studies. We continue to practice and develop our skills, particularly the philosophical skills which I will shortly be telling you about.

I have come to appreciate the way in which my faith has been expanded, nurtured and encouraged from my time with the earth. I am grateful that the walls of my intellectual box have come 'a-tumblin' down.' I have a freedom to imagine and dream and hope in ways I never could have before living in fear and anxiety and shame. I was coming alive.

Chapter 6

Breakthrough

The philosopher Paul Ricoeur talks about stages in our understanding of life. He says that, like little children, we all begin life in a "first naïveté" where we believe what we have been told by those in authority over us. I call this the "God (or parents) said it, I believe it, that settles it for me" stage. In some ways it is a stage of childlike innocence. The second stage is much like adolescence where we begin to question authority and need to make our own choices in what and how we think and believe. Ricoeur calls this the "critical distance" phase. Finally, mature adulthood recognizes that neither of these works. Naïve belief and critical skepticism by themselves tend toward a kind of totalitarian existence. A mature adult is able to hold both together in what Ricoeur called "a second naïveté."

When I was eighteen I had some sort of dream or waking vision in which I was on a 300 foot pillar inside a long circular rock tube that dripped red down the walls. It was hot. I was face down with the devil sitting on my back. He would stroke my back with long fingernails and say "It is hopeless. The father can't save you now. Come with me." And each time he would say this, his fingers would gouge more deeply into my skin to the point it became very painful. At some point I remember the thought entering my head "OK, I will come" and the signal being sent from my brain to my tongue but before the thought became words, quick as a flash, I saw a hand reach out from above and snatch me. I awoke drenched in sweat and shaking with fear. A few weeks later I was "born again."

I have analyzed this many times since. Obviously I was struggling with the direction of my life and it felt like a genuine struggle between good and evil. In some ways, that waking vision has served as a metaphor my whole life. The impact of that vision at age 18 occurred while I was still bound in a first naïveté even though I had begun to move away from my mother's authority toward a critical distance. My immediate sojourn in Christian Fundamentalism reinforced that a first naïveté was 'God's Way.' I simply believed what I was told because God said it was so. It took me two years to engage a 'critical distance' from that tradition.

In my youth and through my Fundamentalist/Evangelical stage I believed in the reality of the demonic. When I was 17 my next door neighbor's parents had gone away for the weekend. Glenn was a 'cowboy' and I was a 'hippie' but we got along well. That weekend he invited two of his cowboy friends over and we decided to go see a movie at the theater. I had no idea how scary *The Exorcist* would be. Neither did the cowboys. That night, all four of us piled in Glenn's mother's bed and slept the night away with the lights on!

My belief in literal demons, reinforced by my waking vision and cemented in a literal reading of Scripture was a real stumbling block for me for years. I was grateful to discover the work of René Girard in my final year of seminary where, for the first time, I realized that the world of the satan and demons were not supernatural but human realities. In the 90's, both through my ministry and in the years after my crash and burn, I struggled with my addictions but refused to anymore do a Flip Wilson "The devil made me do it." I had all sorts of psychological explanations at hand, some of which helped me, some of which didn't. Then I discovered the work of Walter Wink on *The Powers*. Here was a critical thinker who was able to affirm that evil, or the satanic, had a spiritual dimension as well as a human structural form which manifested itself not only in things like hysteria or addiction but also in institutions of oppression or violence. Once again, I began to wonder about all this business of the supernatural. I read a number of books on the history of the devil, where the concept originated and how various cultures and religions understood evil. I still didn't get the whole angel thing though. My intellectual box was still a closed receptacle. If it could not be figured out rationally or logically, I wanted nothing to do with it.

My experiences with spirit-tracking and invisibility didn't fit into any categories I had assembled in my box. It felt uncomfortable leaving them outside as though they were foreigners waiting to cross a national boundary, but I had no choice. They just did not fit. I kept recalling Lorri's epiphany that she finally understood Jesus after taking the first four philosophy classes and so I began to work harder in delving into the gospels and all that entails. Explaining gospel criticism to a person not used to doing it is sort of like explaining brain surgery. Everyone knows what a brain is and everyone knows what surgery is, even so, everyone knows what a gospel is and how criticism works. It is never as easy as it sounds. I can count over a dozen disciplines I must use when I come to a story or saying of Jesus. It is like dissecting a frog only worse. I don't need to dissect frogs but I do need to know what Jesus was saying and what he may have understood or meant by what he said. The deeper I dug, the more I realized I was in a strange new world, a world I could not begin to explain, a world that felt foreign to me. Jesus began to disappear behind the veils of scholarly critique and I would despair.

I wanted so much to return to my Fundamentalist days where everything was black and white but I knew too much to go back down that road. The 'critical' road ahead might as well have been leading to Mordor such was my hopelessness. I could not go forward and I could not go back. I was stuck. So I took my box and placed it

—

on a foundation in my "stuckness" and called that home. I rationalized that I was "living in the mystery" or "living with the tension of reality" but neither of those brought any solace. I met others who had built their homes in the same place. So I wasn't alone. Perhaps there was a subdivision of folks like me who just could not find a way out of their critical distance. It turned out it wasn't a subdivision, or even a city, it was an Empire. I met a few intrepid travelers who had ventured out past the boundaries of The Critical Empire and brought back some new fangled spiritual technique but these never worked for me. They just seemed to produce the warm fuzzies and I wasn't interested in warm fuzzies. I was on a quest for Truth. Like some Don Quixote, I ventured out past the edge of The Critical Empire and heard all kinds of Siren voices. I soon realized that the safety of my little intellectual box in The Critical Empire was preferable to the vast untamed wilderness that led back to Fundamentalism or on to Mordor.

I began reveling in my box becoming a fierce critic to those who lived in Fundamentalist land or the New Age swamps. I was truly stuck between a rock and a hard place. I had no faith of my own and I was sure not going to let anyone else claim they had their own faith. I am certain I became miserable to live with. I knew there was no way to know anything for sure, I also knew others didn't know anything for sure but I still harbored a secret wish that something was truly knowable. I had become a genuine, authentic, real deal 100% Grade-A FDA approved postmodern person. Then came one of my most significant breakthroughs.

In the summer of 2004 I had an opportunity to take three weekend Scout intensives with Tom Brown and a small group of fellow scout trainees. Each of these weekends would prove invaluable both for what I learned and for how I would develop my Scout skills. Sometimes being a Scout can just be plain gross.

In one exercise we were placed in partnerships and my partner was a former Navy Seal, G. He was a real example of why Navy Seals are placed on pedestals of courage. While Tom and a few instructors and volunteers remained in the main area of camp we were to find a way to get to the central fire they were guarding. The problem was threefold: it was broad daylight; there was very little cover once one was within twenty feet of the fire and they had their paintball guns ready to splatter any Scout they saw.

As we got closer to the camp G. came up with an idea that freaked me out. Close to the fire area are several "buildings": a couple of sheds, a woodpile and an outdoor kitchen area. The kitchen is built on top of a platform. G.'s idea was that we would crawl underneath the kitchen platform with its decades of accumulated dust, dirt, and waste that had spilled through the cracks in the flooring. I cannot begin to describe the condition underneath the kitchen. The smell was putrefying; there were plenty of insects and spiders and all manner of gunk. Still G. entered with no fear and I followed as bravely as I could. We made it to the other side of the kitchen and came out behind the tool shed. We were about ten feet from the fire area. Other groups were attempting to come in from various directions and were being fired upon. We drew closer but nobody ever surprises Tom. Splat! We came close but not close enough. I was covered in all manner of filth, yet I learned the value of taking a "road less traveled." *Almost* only counts in horse shoes and hand grenades, but that day it also counted in the paint ball war.

On the weekend of the last intensive Tom had secretly invited a few of us to 'shadow' the rest of the students which meant that while they were out doing their mission, our job was to distract and disrupt them, of course, without ever being seen. We would be in teams of two. So I was completely caught off guard when Tom came to me with a special mission. I was going to go solo. Me? I was just a neophyte in this Scout stuff. It hardly seemed fair but I was excited and honored to be chosen. Little did I know what lay in store.

I applied my camouflage with the most care I have ever done checking myself in the little mirror over and over like some preening peacock. Around 5 pm Tom brought the brown Suburban around and a few 'shadow scouts' climbed in and off we went. He dropped two teams off and then proceeded down the long power line road in the opposite direction from where all the other scouts would be. Several miles down the road he stopped abruptly and said in his gravely voice "Give 'em hell. I will be out there and I don't want to see you or know you are there. Meet me at such and such a place at 10 pm and I will pick you up." That was it. I jumped out of the Burbie and into the brush while Tom drove away. I was sure he had lost his mind. I wasn't a seasoned scout like so many of Tom's students (and they are very, very good). Nevertheless, here I was and I wasn't about to disappoint the master.

Off I went through the brush. I heard a car coming down the power line road and lay low and crawled into a fox run that ran under the brush. At some point I crossed the road and made my way to where I thought the scout groups were heading. All at once the brush broke open before me and I found heaven. It was acres and acres of tall oak trees and pines growing out of a floor of the spongiest moss carpet I had ever laid eyes on. The rays of the early evening sun broke through the leaves and limbs from time to time to create a surreal vision of yellows and greens. It was one of the most astonishing memories I have. I walked slowly on in this Emerald City savoring everything I could. I should have been much more aware than I was but I couldn't help being overwhelmed by the beauty of it all.

Sadly, it didn't last forever and soon I was back in the regular forest brush, which has a beauty all its own. I found tracks from a recent group of four scouts and began following them. As dusk was approaching an eagle swooped down and sat on some tall scrub oak. I didn't know if it was kosher to breathe. I had to keep going while the eagle eyeballed me. Down through the brush I went with the trail off to my right where the scouts had walked. After some time I could hear voices. I had a few tricks up my sleeve (a couple of firecrackers) to scare them. Ahead they turned left onto another road. I knew scouts were to avoid human trails and could not figure out why they were using them. When I came to the main road I crossed it into the deep brush just parallel to the road to follow them when suddenly I found myself on an unused trail that paralleled the road. I knew it was unused by the way it was overgrown and evidenced no human tracks. I decided to use this trail as it would get me closer to the group I wanted to scare. The trail began to diverge slightly from the road but as long as I could keep the sand road on my left I knew I could catch up and overtake them. It diverged more, dusk turned into night and soon the road was long out of sight and I was lost. I suppose I could have backtracked to the road and followed the tracks of the scout group but I had been on that trail for at least twenty minutes and figured I would not be able to catch up with them. I thought I knew where I was but wasn't certain. So I kept going and going. I drank the last of my water. I guessed it was about 8:30 pm or so at least.

At some point I broke through the brush onto another sand road. I waited quietly and listened. I could discern no noise or human presence. I carefully stepped out to the very edge of the brush and saw another sand road intersecting this one about fifty feet ahead. I slowly made my way down to the intersection. Looking right I saw nothing but looking left I could see down about fifty yards what looked like automobile tail lights, dim red in the distance. I got down on my belly and crawled fifty yards. I figured it was Tom waiting for me at the pick up spot but I needed to be able to at least get up to the car unseen. As I got closer I grew more cautious. Closer and closer I came to the Burbie. It seemed to be in the middle of the road which seemed odd and the tail lights were on but I could hear no engine. I could not see past it crawling on my belly. Then it came into view, only it wasn't Tom or the Burbie, it was two tree trunks positioned across the road to make it impassable for cars to pass and had two reflectors on it in case some silly fools came barreling down the road at night. That was when I made my second mistake. My first had been to stick with the meandering trail that got me here in the first place. Now I got scared. It had to be close to 10 pm and I was not where I was supposed to be. Tom would be pissed. Worse, I was lost. Then I heard voices behind me back up by the intersection and in the moonlight I could see a group of four shadows heading into the brush. Quietly I began crawling back. I was afraid if I stood up I could be seen in the moonlight just as I had seen their shadows. But they were my classmates; they could save me from this rotten mess if I could get to them. Maybe I could just shadow them all the way back to camp and as we got close and I knew where I was, then I could scare them.

By the time I made it to the place they entered the brush I could no longer see or hear them. I couldn't track them. I had somehow

70

forgotten everything I learned. I panicked. First I got depressed, then I got angry, really, really angry. I gave up and began stomping down the sand road toward the log barrier. I had no idea where I was, I was getting dehydrated and my emotional state was coming undone. It was not a good place to be. I could see lights off to my right in the distance and thought I could hear the traffic on the Garden State Parkway so I headed that way. Why? I haven't the foggiest idea since it was the opposite direction of camp. Lights maybe? Civilization? This was my third mistake.

I later found that I was wandering toward the nuclear power plant. Not smart for someone all camo'ed up. Somehow I found my way heading in another direction. It had to be after midnight. I was getting really thirsty, I was very tired, and I was hungry, sad, depressed and lost. Then the worse thing possible happened. I found myself in The Maze. The Maze is an incredible area of mixed terrain that Tom uses to teach tracking. But it is called The Maze for a reason. It has all kinds of little sand paths that all wind back in upon themselves. And so it was on a warm August night that I entered Stupidity. I wandered in and out of paths, circled back upon paths, saw my own tracks circling back upon themselves and knew I would be here until morning. I was not a happy camper. Yet, by the grace of some divine pity I eventually found myself on a main sand road. Where it went I could not say. I had no idea where I was. I then made things worse.

My next mistake was to start raging at my situation. The angrier I became at myself, the angrier I became at Tom and the woods and Grandfather and life and every living thing. I stoked the fires of my rage with self-pity until I had a furnace hot enough to melt steel. I began walking or stomping, I wasn't sure. I was fuming. Out in front of me the brush shook hard. As I passed within feet of it I could make out the outline of either the Incredible Hulk or a bear. It was a bear. Either way I was so livid, I just yelled "Get the F@#* out of my way." I stomped on by and eventually found myself at a road with power lines. Could this be The Power Line road that led to camp? I went from anger to hope, walked about a mile, realized it wasn't and sank into The Pit of Despair. It crossed another road with power lines. Now I was really tired and dehydrated. As I walked down that road there came the sweetest sound. I call them banjo frogs. I suppose they have a technical name but when they croak it has a "boing" sound to it. I knew that sound. As I came closer I realized I knew that swamp. I couldn't be more than twenty minutes from camp. I broke into tears.

As I approached camp I was determined to take Tom to task the next morning. It was now around 2:30 am. My partner for the weekend was a Navy Seal just returned from Afghanistan. He was waiting for me by the fire worried that I was out there lost. In between fits of rage and tears I told J. I was going to beat the crap out of Tom when I saw him in the morning which was a really audacious and stupid thing to say inasmuch as Tom is the last person on the planet anyone would want to fight including Superman. He is a lean mean fighting machine capable of leaping tall buildings with a single bound and inflicting all sorts of damage to various body parts.

I eventually made my way to my tent but could hardly fall asleep. The next morning I had risen and was having a cup of coffee waiting for breakfast to be served when Tom came driving into camp. As he exited his car I went up to him and demanded, not asked, but demanded a private conversation with him. We walked a ways away from the rest of the class and I told him how angry I was with him, that the place he told me to meet him didn't exist, that I had followed all the rules and all of the things that had happened to me. It made me angrier to tell him all this as he had this really caring look on his face as he listened. When I was finished ranting and raving he looked at me and barked, "Well, did you learn anything?"

To this day I still go back and reflect on the lessons that night has taught me. Most of all I have learned that I cannot trust my ego to do anything right. It is self-absorbed and fearful. I have learned since then to trust that God loves me dearly and so wherever I am the Love of God is my mantra. I would learn that lesson a few months later.

Chapter 7

Tunnel of Love

I've never been a touchy-feely person. I have not ever really had much use for feelings; they just get in the way. As a child my feelings were whatever my mother told me they were. I am one of those people who hadn't learned how to identify feelings or name them. I knew I had them, I didn't like them, and I didn't want them. Most of all I had no idea about love. The word love for me may as well have been need or dependence or obsession. It had nothing to do with a genuine interest in the other. When people told me God loved me I knew what they meant but it never registered down deep in the core my being. This agape love thing Christians talked about I could affirm in my mind but my heart was closed to it.

I had to keep my heart closed; it was the way I learned to survive. Later in life I would use alcohol and drugs to mask my feelings; and when they weren't available I had "my books and my poetry to protect me" (Paul Simon, *I Am a Rock*). My heart had a "fortress built around it" (Sting) and another one built around that one and another one built around that one. My heart was buried so deep even I couldn't find it. Eventually I gave up looking. I could talk the talk when it came to feelings but I couldn't walk the walk. I learned how to fake the positive ones well enough, the negative ones tended to manifest themselves after half a bottle of scotch.

Maybe Lennon and McCartney were onto something when they sang "All You Need is Love." I wouldn't have known. Like I said, I was not into warm fuzzies. I liked living in my head. Ideas were much better than feelings. Ideas could change the world; feelings were just subjective states to which I had never been.

74

After my last Scout Intensive I made a decision to take the Phil classes that Lorri had taken. Normally a student would take a Philosophy class and then practice for a few years and then take another. I had heard from others how intense they were and Lorri had made it clear that taking Philosophy 1-4 in such a short time was very difficult. There was so much to learn, so many new perspectives to assimilate. Up to that point Tom had offered Philosophy 1-6 and had only run the Philosophy 6 class once previously. That fall he was going to run Philosophy 1-6 and for the first time a Philosophy 7 class. I had no idea how many years down the road before a Phil 7 class would be offered again. So, I did the unthinkable, I signed up for Phil 1-2 in October, Phil 3-4 in November, Phil 5-6 in December and Philosophy 7 in January of 2005. Classmates of mine thought that was absolutely insane. I thought it would be fun. It turned out to be both.

Grandfather had spent his entire life gathering all of the shamanic or spirituality skills from every imaginable Native group in the Americas for over forty years. He traveled on foot from Alaska to Argentina meeting with Native elders and shamans in order to learn the ancient ways. He did this with all of the skills: survival skills, knowledge relating to edible and medicinal herbs, trees and plants, and of course the world beyond the flesh. He then took these skills and distilled them down to their most basic level so that anyone anywhere could master them and join those who had, for centuries, indeed millennia, been able to live with the Earth. Tom would take all of the lessons Grandfather had taught him and create week long classes that further took these skills to a new level. What took Tom months and sometimes years to master he would teach in a week so that with diligent practice a student could also delve into the mysteries of the Creation and the Creator.

In telling the story of my experiences in the Philosophy classes I do not intend to share the techniques I learned. You can learn them by attending classes for yourself or by reading Tom Brown's books, particularly *Grandfather*, *The Journey* and *Awakening Spirits*. It is not my place to put in print what Tom has said better elsewhere or what he and his instructors can teach better than I. Lorri and I have from time to time led groups of laypersons and clergy through weekend retreats where we delve into many of the practices we have learned but it does take an intense time of focus in order to really grasp and utilize these skills. What I can share is how these classes changed my life and how they have helped me to understand Jesus, the earth and the goodness of life. I am a better Christian theologian for having taken these classes. Even though I am now working on my doctorate and still think critically, I can say without reservation I have become a different person as a result of walking not only with Jesus but also with Grandfather.

I am mindful of the warning that Osage George Tinker, who teaches at Illif School of Theology in Denver, insists must be heeded when engaging Native American spirituality. His concern is the way in which white peoples have co-opted Native spirituality to serve their own consumerist ends.[1] Philip Jenkins has examined the history of American consumerism of Native spiritual traditions and documented the case.[2] Grandfather's path is different from the relationship between new age spirituality and native spirituality. Grandfather was following his Vision to learn all the skills he could

---

[1] George Tinker, *Spirit and Resistance: Political Theology and American Indian Liberation* (Minneapolis: Fortress, 2004).

[2] Philipp Jenkins, *Dream Catchers: How Mainstream America Discovered Native Spirituality* (Oxford: Oxford university Press, 2004).

possibly learn, distill them all down to their most basic form while all the time learning from the Earth and the Creator how to thrive and learn in any situation. He then taught his "system" to Tom who is fulfilling Grandfather's vision of teaching it to others. It never ceases to astonish me just how much Tom can teach in a week.

I am not so interested in how to find God; for as a Christian, I believe God has found me. I am interested in being open and willing to learn. I could not have done what Lorri did and jumped right into the Philosophy classes; I would not have been ready for the mind expanding experiences they would bring. I needed to take the route of the survival and scout classes to first break down the walls of my intellectual box.

The Pine Barrens of New Jersey are an oasis in the middle of the state. They are where Grandfather trained Tom and his friend Rick for ten years and where Tom now holds his classes (although he occasionally offers them in California and sometimes Florida). Entering the Primitive Camp where Grandfather taught Tom and Rick, visiting Grandfather's Camp or sit area, walking up on Spirit Hill or venturing into Hell are formidable and wondrous experiences. Every time I enter the Primitive Camp I know that I am in a place that has a certain sacredness attached to it. Not in some weird way but in a genuine sense that here, in this place, lived and worked one of the great persons of the 20th century. As a lover of Karl Barth, René Girard, Dietrich Bonhoeffer and appreciative of the contributions of Dorothy Day, Thomas Merton, Mother Teresa, Dr. King and so many others I can say without a doubt, Grandfather is one of the unsung heroes of my lifetime.

I never met Grandfather, in the flesh. He would have passed on or "gone to the mountain" when I was just entering my teens. Yet, after this past decade I feel I know him as well as I do Barth or Bonhoeffer, Luther or Calvin whose writings I have read for over thirty years. When I first began this venture I even wondered if Grandfather really existed or he was just a figment of Tom's imagination. So I applied the same critical skills that I used to discern the (so-called) 'historical Jesus' in the Gospels to Tom's books and classes. To make a long story short I can say that I have worked out, for myself at any rate, not only that Grandfather existed and that he taught Tom, but also that Tom has faithfully passed on Grandfather's teaching for the most part. I say most part because I have had to learn how to separate Tom from Grandfather, the same way I have learned to separate the authors of the Gospels from Jesus. There is continuity and discontinuity. However, for me, in both cases, the continuity is much greater.

Lorri and I had been partners for a class earlier in the winter of 2004, but since she had already taken Philosophy 1-4, I was on my own for those four classes. Partnering with Lorri has been a huge blessing. Many of my fellow students take classes while their spouses stay home. Since so many exercises require a partner it is difficult to practice outside of class. Lorri and I are able to go back to our notebooks and practice skills together which has not only cemented the bond between us but has also helped us hone our skills.

Tracker School classes begin on Sunday night and run through the following Saturday lunch. Over the years I have learned that Tom speaks in hyperbole. He uses words like epic, or incredible, fantastic or spectacular a little too often for my taste. Still I was surprised when on Sunday night of Phil 1 Tom said that this was the most difficult class for him to teach. "I have to shake loose nothing less than miracles." There was the hyperbole again. I couldn't have been more wrong. There are reproducible results in the Philosophy classes. When Lorri and I have taught workshops we too have seen 'miracles.' What is more amazing is how children can manage to do better than adults with this way of living. They are not as conditioned as we adults are; they have less to risk and are more open to what is being taught. We found this out teaching our granddaughters.

I was not expecting any miracles, but then I had no idea what to expect. If there is one thing I have learned it is that it is best to enter a class with no expectations. One never knows where Tom is going to go in a class. Depending on how well a class is doing he may accelerate the learning curve or decelerate it so that everyone has a chance to grasp and experience what is being taught. Still, I knew from Lorri that this first class was all about meditation and how hard could that be?

I want to emphasize that in talking about the Philosophy 1 class I will not be sharing any "techniques" when I talk about Grandfather's meditation. Tom has already done this in *Awakening Spirits*. If you cannot get to New Jersey to take a class I highly recommend the book or the online courses. Both together are best. Grandfather, you will recall, sought the most effective form of every skill he learned. If the skill could not be practiced by anyone, anywhere, then it was useless knowledge. So, for example, there are over twenty ways to make fire depending on the terrain and weather. Yet if you know two basic ways you can make fire in almost any circumstance. There are scores of ways to make a shelter, yet a debris hut built properly can keep one snug and warm in almost any condition. So it is with the entry into the meditation Grandfather taught. There have been many meditation techniques from all over the world that have taught for

—

many thousands of years. Almost all of them involve a focused attention to silence. For Grandfather, too many meditation techniques amounted to little more than navel gazing or a form of 'spiritual masturbation.' They were ego-centric and self-serving. Meditation, in many forms seems all about the self and how one could connect to all life rather than realizing one was already connected to all life and how to live in that life.

I had tried meditating when I went through my Jungian phase back in the 1980's while I was in seminary. I found it impossible. Nothing could quiet all of the voices and music that ran through my head. Try as I might to achieve some sort of internal bliss, meditation only produced more and more frustration so eventually I gave it up. Getting stoned produced more inner calm than meditating.

It was, therefore, with some misgiving that I went to Philosophy 1. I figured I could pretend and bypass all of the meditation nonsense to get to Philosophy 2. There would be two important aspects to that first philosophy class. The first was our personal sit spot; the second the meditation in which we would engage.

A sit spot is an area in the woods (or your backyard) where you go on a regular basis and become quiet and one with the earth. A sit spot is the place where you learn how to gauge the baseline of your sit area and how all of life interacts in that area. We would use our sit spots regularly, several times a day. It is a rare class that one does not have a sit spot.

The second aspect to the class was learning the form of meditation that Grandfather taught Tom and Rick. It is first learned in its long form. It begins with relaxation, then a visualization process that includes a path, some stairs that go down to an arch through which one enters a medicine area and finally ends up in a 'sit spot' in the world of the spirit also known as one's own personal sacred area. That is it at its simplest. We would lie on our sleeping bags in the dining hall of the Boy Scout camp and do this time and again, each time being able to "see" more and more of the path, stairs, arch, medicine and sacred areas. It was difficult at first for I found my visualization shifting. Sometimes the ground was firm; sometimes it was more like sponge cake. At first my path was dark, later it would lighten up. My arch changed many times. I thought maybe I was doing something wrong. After time, as I became more focused things became sharper and clearer.

One of the inhibitors to my meditation was my theological box. I simply did not want to engage in some new age nonsense. As far as I was concerned most new age stuff was just hippie-dippy bullshit. It lacked any intellectual sophistication or grounding in the rational structure of the universe as I knew it. So when we first began the meditations I was going through an internal dialogue. "Is this stupid or what? Be quiet and just do it! But why? I can't believe I paid good money to be lying on a floor. This is stupid. Shhhh. Just play the game, its OK. What's OK about it? What if this is really not good? What if it's demonic? What if the Fundamentalists are right? What if it's just me projecting? What if…? Shhh. It wouldn't hurt to try it out, you don't have to believe in it, just go along for the ride and see what happens. You can always throw it out."

So I went along and it got easier. But no way was I going to throw my Christian faith out the window, so by the time I got to my arch the first time I made sure it had a cross at the top. I made damn sure I took Jesus with me on this journey. This worked OK for a while, then at some point during the week as I descended the steps to the arch I noticed my archway had changed and the cross was no longer there. Instead, inscribed in the stone at the top of my arch (which previously had been wooden) was Hebrew script that read 'Baruch ha Adonai' (Blessed be the Lord). That was strange. I didn't know what to make of it. Maybe it meant I had to be Jewish or something. I was circumcised, would that help me?

We learned a lot of different things that week; meditations occupied a good part of our time but not all of it. We made our own medicine pipes, learned about herbal mixtures, Inner Vision, the importance of need, passion and faith, and the realms beyond our physical world. The meditations, however, provided the grist for everything else we did. I haven't counted the number of times we lay on our sleeping bags that week while Malcolm or Larry or Tom took us down the path and stairs, through the arch and into the medicine and sacred areas. It felt like a hundred but it was probably more like fifteen or twenty. By Friday night I felt like it had become much easier than when I began on Monday and I was quite pleased. The next morning we would do our final meditation before class was over.

Saturday morning was a beautiful autumn day. I had made friends with Sarge that week. Sarge's life consisted of nothing but the military. He loved being out in the field with "his men." We both had a good time mocking the sissiness of meditating although we were careful to do it quietly. Lorri was due to come and meet me at 1:00 pm. We planned on camping out at the Boy Scout camp together before she would turn around the next afternoon and head home while I would go on to begin the Philosophy 2 class.

Tom gave his last lecture and it was time for our last meditation. Once again we lay down on our sleeping bags. Once again we closed our eyes and relaxed. Once again we began our walk down the path. Our destination changed and a little later I found myself in a tunnel. Somehow there was just light enough for me to see. Way off in the distance I could make out a light at the end of the tunnel. I headed for it. When I arrived at the edge of the tunnel there felt like a clear demarcation between the tunnel and the light beyond. I didn't realize I was not supposed to pass this boundary. I just kept going and stepped across as if this had been my destination the whole time. At no other time during a meditation had I lost awareness that I was lying on the floor of the Boy Scout Camp dining hall. When I crossed the threshold into the light it became all I knew at that moment. It was an overwhelming brightness but it didn't seem to hurt my eyes. I could make out a large step and some colonnades both made of light and a floor, like a huge temple area made of light but that was all I could see. Then I heard a voice that uttered five little words.

"There is no fear here."

Suddenly, for the first time in my life, I felt an overwhelming love pour through my entire body; my whole being was infused with something so precious, so beautiful, and so wondrous. I could hardly breathe yet I could breathe for the first time. Love so extraordinary, the magnificence, the grandeur of it, the splendor of it took me. I have no idea if I was there for a second, a minute or a lifetime. Without warning I found myself back across the threshold looking in and turning around to come back down the tunnel.

I finished the meditation but was stunned. What had I just experienced? Was it for real? How could I even begin to describe it? Shortly thereafter class ended. I walked over to Sarge. He asked how

I was doing and I started bawling. Not little manly sobs, but all out crying, sobbing, tears and all that girlie stuff. Sarge put his arms around like we had just lost our best friend on the battlefield and held me as I soaked his shirt and neck with my tears. I know at one point we went outside where we continued our session, me crying, Sarge just being a big brother. I must have let out forty-eight years of tears. When I finished I felt cleansed. And for the first time I knew what it meant to be loved.

Chapter 8

"All Things Are Possible"

Jesus did miracles. At least that seems to be the perspective of the Gospel writers and the early church. Miracles were the purview of God. They were supernatural acts, things well beyond the ordinary. Jesus turned the water into wine. This was no cheap trick. It's not like he turned water into some cheap four-dollar-a-bottle-stuff a wino would drink. No this was fine wine, some special vintage cabernet with an oak palette and a buttery finish. He also made the blind to see, the lame walk and the deaf to hear. He walked on water. Jesus was a miracle worker.

When I was in my first naïveté as a Fundamentalist/Evangelical I was told that Jesus could do miracles because he was God. His human nature of course was quite limited; so anything that wasn't normal must have come from God. We could not do miracles, of course, because we were human. At first I was taught that miracles were only for a certain limited time to validate the apostolic message of the gospel, after that Greek philosophy did just fine. A little later when I began hanging around more charismatic type folks I was told that The Holy Ghost gave certain people the ability to heal others. The proof was in the way God blessed Oral Roberts and other televangelists. Just put your hand on your TV set, send in $50 and you too could be healed. I figured it was as good a scam as any shell game on the street.

In my critical distance years I knew that there was no such thing as miracles. The gospel writers may have thought Jesus was doing something supernatural but everything could really be explained by Jesus' great power of suggestion or some other psychological trick. Natural laws could not be broken and that was that. Besides did anyone really have proof that miracles could happen nowadays? No one I knew had ever seen or met someone who had spent three days in a morgue only to come back to life, and if they did I'm pretty sure we would be in the thick of a zombie invasion right now. Nobody in their right mind wants someone to return from the dead, all they want is your brain.

Tom said he had to get miracles in Philosophy 1. I don't recall any gospel-like miracles but after Lorri left that Sunday afternoon and I took a walk waiting for Philosophy 2 to begin later that night I thought about what had happened to me when I walked into the light. It had changed me. I felt something I had never felt before. I felt loved. That was enough of a miracle for me. I would tear up every time I thought about those words I had heard "There is no fear here." Could it really be that whatever lies beyond mortality is truly life and love and peace?

In Philosophy 2 we expanded on our meditation practice. This would lead me to two lessons that are imprinted on my soul to this very day. The first is that we are called to be genuine healers of one another and the earth. Life lived apart from being willing to heal our relationships and others is a fruitless life. The second also had to do with something I was sure did not exist until I came face to face with it: the dark side.

Both healing and the dark side are woven into the story of Jesus as told in the Gospels. I have already mentioned Jesus' healings. The gospels are full of them. One aspect of Jesus' healings I have always found important is not their so-called 'supernatural' aspect but the fact, as some biblical scholars have pointed out, that when Jesus healed someone he set them free from being marginalized so they could rejoin human society. Healing in Jesus' ministry was a form of re-socialization or re-humanizing the marginalized. It was not as though Jesus pranced about saying "Look at me, I'm a healer. La, La, La. God is with me, I have power and you don't, Na, na, na, na, na." The opposite was true. Like any real, genuine healer (shaman), Jesus hushed up that side of his ministry. He did not start a mega-synagogue replete with crutches on the wall and a souped-up sound system. When he healed he asked those he healed to keep it quiet. Healers (shaman) don't go around advertising themselves because healing has nothing to do with the ego.

The gospels are also full of Jesus' battle against the dark side. The gospels open with the great sequence of Jesus' baptism, being filled with the Holy Spirit and then being driven into the desert to be tested by the satan. They are filled with stories of Jesus exorcising evil from the lives of people in bondage; and they end with that great temptation in Gethsemane where Jesus would be tested to in fact, pick up the sword in order to defend himself. What scholars call the apocalyptic structure of the gospels (or even of Jesus' message), that great battle of good vs. evil runs throughout the gospel narratives. In short, Jesus knew the dark side, did battle against the dark side and conquered the dark side. Humans have a dark side.

Going all the way back to Greek philosophy, we have sought to construct maps of the human being. The ancient Greek philosophers beginning with Plato taught that humans were composed of a body, a soul and a spirit. Some believed that the soul was eternal and when a baby was born the soul would come down from heaven and inhabit the body and upon death the soul would return to the divine. This was pretty much the way we understood what it was to be human until the advent of modern psychology. Sigmund Freud altered the landscape of how we understood ourselves with his map of the human mind which consisted of an ego, the id and the superego. Carl Jung would go further and speak of the Self, the anima/animus, the shadow, and the persona. Other great psychologists would create their own maps of the mind. In our own time we are seeing how the brain-mind dichotomy has broken down and we are learning to map the brain and talk of mind-brain integration.

Grandfather also had a map of the human. When I first encountered it I was a little bit shocked at what it contained, then I was in awe at how comprehensive it was. My work in anthropology, psychology and related studies had both prepared me and not prepared me for what I was about to learn. Philosophy 2 would become a class that continued to demand that I open the walls of my little intellectual box which by now was becoming quite small to me. I was ready to explore outside the limits of what I knew.

Like all maps, Grandfather's map is not the territory. It is simply a useful tool to help one become acquainted with one's self in relation to one's self, others, the creation and God. It is a map that would eventually be integrated and transcended. But in the beginning it was a necessary map. For Grandfather, humans share in the possibility of several spheres or aspects of life. There is the physical which we are all familiar with for it includes our body and five senses. Now, unlike Greek philosophy which has the soul inside the body and the spirit buried even further inside the soul, Grandfather suggested that the body or the physical is the innermost circle of human existence. The next sphere or circle or area beyond the physical Tom and Rick called "The Force." I know, that sounds like Star Wars. If one thinks of force as energy then the word is appropriate. I prefer to use the term "Life Force" when I teach about this thinking in terms of the

---

Hebrew word *'nephesh"* which is the animating reality of life. In Genesis 2 God takes the *adama*, the clay, breathes into the clay 'spirit' (*ruach*) and the human becomes a living *nephesh*.

Beyond the sphere or circle of the Life Force is the world of spirit. Trust me, when I first heard this I didn't believe it either. Beyond the circle or area of the spirit is the place Tom would call The Void, which was reserved for the Creator. I have since wondered if the Bible doesn't somehow reference a similar metaphor when it speaks of "a glass sea, like crystal" in front of the throne of God where the higher spirits like cherubim and seraphim dwell (Rev 4). This does not exhaust Grandfather's map but I wouldn't know that until years later.

"The map is not the territory, it is only a tool." It was essential for me to keep this in mind as my internal skeptic would not keep quiet. How much simpler and more reasonable were the mind-maps of Freud, Jung, Adler or Horney. I wasn't sure if I could buy into this spirit world stuff and I thought for sure Tom had ripped off Star Wars for the 'Force.' I had read in one of Tom's books that living in the Force was a human birthright but I suspected that I had experienced all the good stuff in Philosophy 1 and that this class was going down the slippery slope into bullshit, new age or otherwise.

If we were meant to live in the Life Force (or *nephesh*) and it was our human birthright what exactly was it for and how do we access it? This is where the meditation became a vehicle for me to enter into another world. Tom talks about the Force in his book *The Journey* and gives numerous examples of his own failures and successes there as he was taught by Grandfather. For argument's sake let's assume that such a thing exists. I can't prove it and I wouldn't want to try. I

—

have chosen to dwell there literally thousands of times, indeed daily now since then, and have learned how to use it for healing, telepathic communication and other things.

For example, if you can find it plausible to believe with Carl Jung that there is such a thing as a 'collective unconscious' then you can also accept that we humans have access to each other's minds. In other words, there is a 'human Internet.' The sad reality is that while we are all typing frantically away at our mental/spiritual keyboards, even in our dreams, very few have their internal monitors turned on.

How we access the collective unconscious for Jung occurred in dreams. In mirror neuron research we have evidence that the human brain can perceive intention. We could sense things about each other long before we knew them. In the Force it is possible to send and receive data with another person. Images are easier than words (at least in my experience). Lorri and I have practiced this frequently. She has a habit of leaving the house without our cell phone when she goes to the store. That's good because she can't talk while she drives. It is bad when I remember something else we need at the store. Through Force communication I could send her a picture of something we needed and she would receive it. When we are apart we practice sending one message a day to each other. We write it down so we can compare what was sent with what was received. Sometimes when she is traveling and is late I ask her where she is and she replies. When she returns we debrief on the message I sent and her response. Many worries have melted away because I knew she had gone to another store and would be home later than she planned. Once when I was in Holland for two weeks we wanted to find out if distance mattered. Just like 'spooky action at a distance' in quantum physics, it didn't.

Sending and receiving is easier than you might think. It is also potentially very dangerous to married men. In one class we were sent out as a partnership to a trail system that had many intersecting trails. I was to be the receiver so I stood about eight feet in front of Lorri and she was to "steer" me from behind. Each time I came to a fork in the trail where I could go right or left, I would take a breath to surrender, "listen" to where Lorri wanted me to go and take the turn. She was only to stop me if I turned the wrong way so we could figure out how we could improve our "force communication." So off I went, taking turn after turn. We had done quite a few turns as I recall when she burst out laughing hysterically behind me. I turned around to find her doubled over in an uncontrollable fit of laughter. It took her a minute before she blurted out "You're so steerable" to which I replied "I am so screwed. If I find myself at home mopping the floor, polishing the furniture, doing the laundry and mowing the lawn I'll know you have gone to the dark side!"

Sometimes in the gospels the writers say that Jesus knew what certain people were thinking. Until I learned how to send and receive I thought that was a lot of hullaballoo. Now I would say Jesus was simply living his potential as a full and complete human being which included dwelling in the Life Force.

It would be easy for me to take all of this for granted, much easier still for me to use this to my own advantage or gain. When one discovers that all things are possible, how easy is it to read another person's mind without their knowing or to put a thought into someone's mind so they would do your will? To violate the integrity of the other was to go to the dark side. Tom could not stress enough how once we learned how to live in the Force we were never, ever, under any circumstance to use it for our own profit or gain. I thought it was more overkill and Tom was just being his usual hyperbolic self.

Was it possible that I, a reasonably decent Christian, well maybe not that good, but at least trying in my own feeble way to follow Jesus, could turn to the dark side? Could I imagine using this power to get my will done, to force my will on another unsuspectingly? Not me, surely not me. But I was as blind as Peter who claimed he would never, ever betray Jesus.

I had quit believing in hell or the devil or demons two decades previous. Sleeping with the cowboys after watching *The Exorcist* was just a faded memory. *That* was probably scarier than any demon that might have popped out from under the bed. My worldview box was secure in the knowledge that spiritual reality did not include a dark side. In fact reality probably did not include a spiritual component, so "What, me worry?"

I could rationalize anything away with the best of them. It wasn't just my theological training that helped in this regard; it was also my addictive personality. Combined they were a powerful tool of denial. I was good at denial, really good. If I didn't like something I would just deny its existence and therefore it wasn't there. People that thought otherwise were just ignorant, stupid or hoodwinked. So it was with hell. I hadn't become a full fledged Universalist believing that everybody went to heaven, but I certainly had no room for hell in my theology. What I would later find out was that I had no room for a punishing god in my theology, a god who mercilessly tortured people endlessly just to stroke his ego. I was to soon find out, however, that hell was very real and even worse than I imagined.

.

———

92

Only it was not anything like the place I had been told about by the church or the theologians.

There is a Hell, Michigan. It was built by nearby Hell creek and was owned for a while by someone named George Reeves. Greek mythology has its Hades, Jewish apocalyptic has its Gehenna. Christian theology has its hell as well. Other religions also have a place for torment after death. The Pine Barrens in New Jersey also has a Hell and there is also a Hell in the spirit world. I slammed into it one day. It wasn't pretty.

We had been learning about the importance of using our skills to heal, help and aid others. There was no point in using them selfishly. If that happened we would no longer be children of light but we would start down the path to becoming children of darkness. Power is like Sauron's ring: it consumes your every thought. Once you have a taste of it you can only want more. Possessing power is the greatest human addiction there is; its appetite can never be sated. More is always better. So we were warned over and over again to be very careful, we were constantly challenged to make a commitment to the good, the true, and the beautiful, as it were.

What might happen to us if we chose darkness? Could we imagine? Could we see what our future looked like if we chose darkness instead of light? It was time to have a go at another meditation. Path, stairs, arch, medicine area, sacred area. Then what was this? I was led down a trail beyond a Great Veil into the realm of the spirit world. Looming ahead was a black wall, as though made of solid obsidian. As we got closer I could see faces in the wall, faces in extreme distress and agony, frozen in pain and anguish, seeking relief and release and behind the dead eyes knowing there would never be any exodus from this blackness. I felt sorry for them, for these were the people who had made a choice for darkness. Then I saw something that disturbed my vision. I recognized a face in that Wall. Who was it? Who did I know that had turned to everlasting darkness and was now paying a price too great for any soul to bear? I got as close as I dared and saw that it was my own face. I wanted to scream, to cry out, "Not me, it wasn't me, I don't belong here. No, NO!"

When the meditation ended I knew I was seeing only a possible future, something that was neither destined to happen nor had happened, but one that could happen if I made a choice to use my skills selfishly. Like Jesus in the wilderness, I have had to confront the darkness that would test me to provide my own safety, security and comfort instead of trusting my heavenly *Abba*. How often I have wanted to know the winning lottery numbers, how often I have had to let that temptation pass and be assured that I am deeply loved by the Creator of all life. Like Jesus, I have had to battle my own hell and darkness and like Jesus, and because of his example I have been able to come out on the side of light. It is a constant battle. But the apostle Paul has admonished us to "resist the devil." So I do.

One day the light will shine in the darkness everywhere. Until that day all I can do is be the best light I can be in the midst of the darkness around me.

Chapter 9

Presence

I have often heard Christians talk about the presence of God in their lives. I have also used this language. Usually I tend to think of God's presence as a very generic thing. When good things happen or when I feel blessed by someone or something, I say it is God's presence. If it is good, it must be God. The Jewish Scriptures refer to "God's presence" going with the people of Israel. This is another term for God's *shekinah* or *glory*.

The presence of God seems elusive. Jesus said "I will be with you always" by which I would have to say on the face of it means that he is present with us. His being present means that his presence is with us. However we may understand the presence of God or Jesus in our lives, I was astonished to learn that everything has presence.

Grandfather taught Tom and Rick that all created reality has presence, its own unique presence. This presence could be detected. Learning the ins and outs of presence took me quite a while. Presence is like a field of energy around an object. One term that has been used for presence is aura. Objects have energy fields that some people can see thus an aura. When I first heard this I was quite skeptical. I had not yet gotten around to thinking Grandfather's philosophy through in terms of quantum mechanics or the discipline known as quantum theology. What convinced me was Kirilian photography. The best way to get a grasp of this is to Google pictures of it. On the Internet you will find hundreds of photos of all sorts of objects, animate and inanimate, that under the special conditions of Kirilian photography have an energy field around them. Some of these pictures are rather beautiful.

Everything emits some sort of energy or radiation. On a hot day you can see heat radiating from the pavement and causing a shimmering effect as it rises. So too, we humans emit radiation, heat or energy. That is not all we emit but we shall leave *those* things unsaid. Some emissions are prettier than others. Presence is the radiation that comes, not just from the physical, but also from the Force and the spirit. It is a combination of all three thus it is the energy field emitted by the whole object or the whole person. It cannot be detected on a purely physical level, nor simply in the Life Force or spirit; it is a combination of all three and so must be detected by an equal balance of all three.

I admit that I was not convinced. OK, so I had spirit tracked a fox but other than that I had no real hard empirical proof of any of this force or spirit stuff. It still felt a bit spooky to me. I would occasionally tune Tom out as he was teaching just to be sure I wasn't being hypnotized. Still, as before, Grandfather had given Tom and Rick exercises that would demonstrate, to my critical mind, the 'reality' of presence. Today it has become one of the most useful tools I possess when I speak to groups or pray for someone. Let me tell you a few stories.

When Lorri and I run workshops we teach people how to detect presence using the same exercises we used in class. We have also taught our granddaughters and found that young people and teenagers are really adept at this. That is because they have less to unlearn and still have imaginations. Not that this is fantasy, but imagination is the ability to think outside the intellectual box.

On my bathroom sink I have an assorted collection of sticks, rocks and shells. It makes for a nice little display. Gather one stick, one rock, one seashell and a partner. The next part is important and should not be rushed. Take one of the items in your hand and close your eyes. Now deep within yourself surrender all thought. Surrender to nothingness. You are surrendering your logical or rational mind. What you think is not important in this exercise, it is all about what you sense deep within. It is about what we might say is listening to your heart or Inner Vision. Each item, say the shell, has its own energy or presence. You cannot detect it on the physical level which is why you must surrender your mind to your heart.

As you surrender feel the sense of presence emitted by the shell, stick or rock. Do it again until you have an awareness of the deeper sense within yourself. Repeat this with the other two objects. This is where you will notice a difference between them. Different people experience presence in different ways. There is no one right way to do it. For some it comes as a feeling, for others an image, still for others a word. Your way is your way. After you have taken time to do this take a blindfold and put it on yourself. Now have your partner quietly place the stick, rock or shell on the table in front of you and take your hand and hold it over the object. Do not touch the object. Surrender and listen. The first sense or image or word you get say out loud. You are connected to all life energy on all the levels of the flesh, force and spirit, and together you will know what that object is. Repeat this over and over again with all three objects.

I have watched as people get six, eight, ten or more "hits" in a row. Why does it work for some and not for others? Why didn't it work for me the first time I did this exercise? Because I was listening to my mind. Oh, I think it must be the rock they will start with or they have done the stick and the rock so now it is the shell's turn. At a certain point I realized I was just guessing while hoping to beat the

—

odds. As long as I allowed my mind to play games with me, as long as I had not truly surrendered, I could not even begin to get it right. The first time I truly let go and listened deep within, I "hit" the correct answer time and again.

One time Lorri and I had a youth group on a weekend retreat where we sought to show them the awesome power God had given to all humans, not just to Jesus. We had brought some shells with us and had the teens gather some sticks and rocks from outside. One particular partnership, two girls, had "hits" (correct answers) for over a dozen times in a row then all of a sudden they could not get anything right. They were completely baffled why this was so. I asked them if they felt confident that they could get it right every time. "Of course," they said. I pointed out to them that what was prohibiting them from discerning the presence of the stick, rock or shell were their egos. They had become seduced by their success and so their surrender was no longer a genuine surrendering. Once they understood this and let go of their ego they were once again able to identify the presence of the stick, rock and shell.

Another way to determine presence is a game we play with our granddaughters. We blindfold one of us and stand in the middle of our living room. That person plugs their ears and counts to twenty. This gives the other three time to find a place in the room to stand or sit quietly. When the person blindfolded has reached twenty they unplug their ears and surrender all thought and slowly rotate around in a full circle seeking to determine the presence of each person. As they are able to detect them they point at them and identify them. "That's Grandpa" or "That's Laurelin." They do this until they have "found" all three persons. It is a fun game for a rainy or snowy day.

—

98

There are two elements to presence: identity, which I have just given examples of, and intent. Animals are very good at discerning intent. When you come home the dog senses your mood and acts accordingly. So too, in the wild, animals have evolved to discern the intent in presence so they can survive. Obviously some are better at it than others.

Have your partner stand about twenty feet in front of you facing away from you. Doing this on a carpet helps but I suggest removing your shoes if you are on a floor. A lawn is great for this. Make sure to remove anything from your body that will jingle or jangle, especially coins or keys in your pocket as you are going to stealthily stalk your partner. The person being stalked is to surrender and dwell in the silence of the heart. The person behind will quietly begin to move forward. The partners will have agreed beforehand that when the stalking person is three feet behind the person being stalked the person being stalked will raise a hand. The person stalking should have a quiet heart and mind thinking of nothing, just moving toward the other partner with no intent, good or bad. Do this repeatedly switching roles until both partners have a sense of when the other partner is x number of feet away (it doesn't have to be three, it could be four or six depending on how much room one has to stalk).

Here is a question: have you ever felt like someone was looking at you or watching you? Did you turn to see who it was? Have you ever been walking in a big city at night and felt like you had to have your internal radar on full blast? Most of us have some experiences like this. This is because we are picking up intent. If we are in a state of awareness and someone intends to hurt us we can feel it.

Take your partner again and repeat the exercise as before with this twist: Agree beforehand that at some point during your stalk your intent will change from benign to one of malice. I like to pick an area on my partner's back and with my imaginary knife or bow and arrow intend to hurt them. You cannot fake this; it must be as real an emotion as you can make it. The person being stalked will then raise a hand at the moment you change your intent. You may be twenty feet behind them, ten feet or three feet. It doesn't matter. It is when your intent changes that the other partner should raise a hand. The person being stalked must remember to surrender and dwell there, and may need to intentionally surrender to nothingness two or three during the stalking.

These are some basic exercises for discerning presence. They can get really complex. One time Lorri and I were to go to each other's sit areas and change one thing, maybe move a rock or remove a twig. We were then to sit in our own sit area, surrender and determine what had been changed. Everything has presence, so when you add or remove something, the presence changes. You have probably experienced this when you were hanging out with another person or a few friends. As a couple or as a group you have a certain presence. When another person enters the group, the presence of that group changes as it does when someone leaves. So, you can detect presence. Grandfather taught Tom to be aware at all times of presence. Our "presence detection meter" is like a rheostat which we can turn up or down. When I am sitting in a park or taking a walk in the woods I intend my "presence rheostat" to be set to just below mid range. If I am walking in Manhattan at night or in scout mode, I have it set much higher (usually Def Con 5) so I can discern trouble before it happens and avoid it.

Evil also has a presence. I cannot say that I have ever met anyone I would say is truly evil yet, but I have been places where the presence of evil lingered. I will never forget the first concentration camp I visited, Bergen-Belsen. It was the Nazi concentration camp in which Anne Frank died in March 1945. There is something creepy about concentration camps. In many of them the first thing you enter is a museum detailing the atrocities committed. The photos of the extermination of European Jewry, and others, take the human heart to a place it would rather not go. Some people have felt it around Ground Zero in New York City, others by walking in the Killing Fields of Cambodia. I really felt it walking the battlefield of Gettysburg, Pennsylvania. Sadly, there are far too many of these kinds of places on the planet.

The problem of evil is a complex subject. Why is there evil in the world? Why does a good God allow evil? Why do people do evil things to other people? I have scores of books in my library that discuss these and other questions. In *The People of the Lie*, psychologist M. Scott Peck marshals evidence for a profile of an evil person. But evil is not always ugly. When Hannah Arendt went to observe the trial of Nazi Adolf Eichmann in Israel she was struck by his responses that he was just following orders. She referred to the "banality of evil." Evil can take many forms, it can be ugly like the torturers in the Quentin Tarantino film *Hostel* or it can be disguised as righteousness as when a group of homophobic young men lynch a gay person. America is replete with examples of "righteous evil." As the apostle Paul says, the satan can be disguised as an angel of light.

I work with a simple definition of evil: evil is that which destroys life. Evil is opposed to life. God is a life-giver; evil is a life-taker. We can all participate in evil. We don't have to murder someone in cold blood to act in an evil manner. We can participate in evil when we suck the life out of a relationship, when we accuse the innocent, when we condemn others different than ourselves. For some people life can be hell.

One night in Philosophy 3 we went to Hell, that area in the Pine Barrens that Grandfather and Tom use as a teaching tool. Hell has a history. It is ground soiled with the blood of innocents. It has been a place of satanic ritual and it has been used as a burial ground for criminal enterprises. Our class was to go to a number of 'sacred' places and do a meditation. One of those places was Hell. If each place has its own aura or presence Hell certainly has its own. It just feels neglected. One does not find many animal tracks in Hell; it is as if the animals avoid it, and rightly so. At night it has that feel of a haunted house, as though something is lying in wait. We all knew that Tom had faced "The Stalker" of Hell. He talks about it in one of his books. It was a terrifying experience for him.

Now darkness has many tools but the greatest of them is fear. As a Christian I believe that Hell has been harrowed, conquered, overcome and emptied. This was the view of the early church. Jesus in his death has exposed the principalities and powers (Col 2:12-15) and, according some traditions, after his death, went to Hell and broke down its gates and led humanity out of the grip of the satan and darkness. Nevertheless, as we walked up the firebreak to our place of meditation I could discern a very real presence that was not goodness or light, it was something else altogether.

We sat down as a class and began our meditation. The darkness of the night amplified the darkness of the place. I sat with a quiet mind and heart and then suddenly saw a dark caped figure coming toward the group. What was this? Could I be hallucinating or projecting?

Perhaps. Perhaps I was actually seeing/sensing something else. Our group then dispersed so that we were no longer in a protective circle. I picked a spot a ways away from others and turned so I could not see anyone, only the darkness of the forest.

After a few minutes the ground began to beat bright red, as though I was seeing the beating heart of hell. For some reason Psalm 22 came to my mind. Psalm 22 is about the victimization of the innocent. I sensed the presence of innocent life snuffed out for no reason at all in this unholy place. I could "hear" screaming and crying, pleading and begging. Out of the darkness wild dogs jumped at me, snarling and dripping saliva from their fangs. I held my ground and refused to look away, I refused to be afraid. They seemed to melt away in mid-leap. It was then I began to recall the horrors of the Nazi death camps and the hell that had been created on earth in Eastern Europe. I knew that hell existed, that it was created by humans and that its only power was human power: power for destruction and death.

November in the Pine Barrens is cold; Hell in November has its own kind of coldness. It is the coldness of death. According to the apostle Paul, death is the enemy. We humans were not meant to know death. But we do. Death is all around us. We do not want to acknowledge it; we are in *Denial of Death* as Ernst Becker says. Yet every time we hear of random innocents being slaughtered we cannot but be aware of this enemy. Every school shooting or mall or theater shooting, every casualty of war, every innocent child abused reminds us that while evil in some forms may be banal, in other forms it is atrocious.

The Philosophy 3 class left me with more questions than answers. I knew that the writer to the Ephesians spoke of the battle we engage against the dark side and wondered about that all weekend while I waited for Philosophy 4 to begin.

Sometimes there is more to a thing than meets the eye.

Chapter 10

Entering the Fray

I spent that weekend ruminating on this business of evil. Due to my work in René Girard's mimetic theory and with the help of certain psychologists I have long since abandoned the idea of a "personal" devil. Many Christians believe the devil is a fallen angel. One does not find this in the Bible; it has to be imported from a way of thinking found in pre-Christian Judaism. Several hundred years before Jesus, certain Jewish thinkers conceived of a great battle in heaven. Satan and many of his "generals and lieutenants" were cast out of heaven. Most of them were cast straight down to hell. In the book known as I Enoch, the demons plead to God not to send all of them to hell so God relents and leaves ten percent of them to roam the earth and cause trouble for humanity. This has become the default position for many Christians, especially for those who read the Bible literally or still think of the modern world in medieval terms.

On the other side are those who deny the existence of the devil. Evil is a purely human phenomenon. There is no spiritual dark side. Everything evil can be explained through psychology or sociology or some other human science. This would seem to be the default position of the rational thinking person who was not religious. It does not have to be an either–or decision.

Discovering the work of Walter Wink on The Powers, especially his book *Engaging the Powers* has helped me to frame the question of the spiritual and evil in new ways that does not get bogged down in either religious naïveté or empirical skepticism. Wink is able to show that, from the perspective of the Bible, the very same language used for institutions of oppression (like the state) could also be used of spiritual realities of darkness. He says that every physical reality has its spiritual side. I have often wondered why the modern anti-war movement lacked such power while Dr King's civil rights movement had such power. It occurs to me that the anti-war movement or the peace movement or the green earth movement all seek change on the purely physical level. Dr King brought change by addressing the spirituality of racism. His movement did not just hold vigils or marches. These marches and vigils were worship services that announced to the 'principalities and powers' that there was another greater Lord and Master of the universe who was love and light and who conquered darkness in all its forms.

So, like Dr. King and Walter Wink, Grandfather also talked about the *duality* of the human, of the physical and the spiritual. He did not speak of *dualism*, as though the physical and spiritual were not related but of the two-fold interconnectedness of the physical and spiritual realities. There is great power when both sides of the human problem are addressed. If we only focus on the spiritual side we end up, like some, practicing some over the top silly deliverance ministry where there seems to be a demon behind every bush. If we focus only on the physical side of structural evil, we are not really getting to the heart of the battle and so our protestations fall on deaf ears.

Philosophy 4 was about power. Just as evil is a power and acts powerfully, so also one needs to respond to evil with power. Power does not mean force or violence. This is a common mistake. We sometimes think we can fight evil with bullets, tanks and bombs. This is a strategy destined for failure. Viet Nam should have awakened our Defense Department to that. In our own time one must ask what good it does to fight against an idea with guns and armies.

How does one conduct a war on 'terror' if all one does is terrorize back, using 'Shock and Awe' tactics. Have we really won the wars in Iraq and Afghanistan? Not really. A decade since those wars began all we have managed to produce are two countries that are in worse shape than when we went in with our great American military might. Had we used a different kind of power, had we addressed the spiritual roots of the conflict, had we sought to be peacemakers and country builders perhaps things would have turned out differently.

The writer to the Ephesians when speaking of spiritual warfare says we are to "Be empowered by the Lord and his powerful power" (Eph. 6:10 my translation). You cannot do battle against evil in the flesh, on a purely physical level; it takes another source of power, the power of light and love, of mercy and compassion, of justice and truth. This is why the writer goes on to describe the armor that one must wear when going forth into battle. This armor includes truth, justice, and peace and a redemptive message. Like any soldier learning to do battle, training begins with learning the tools of one's craft.

Grandfather had many teaching tools. One of them was the blindfold. We used a blindfold for scores of exercises. Being blindfolded takes the focus off of the physical and shifts one into the world of the Life Force and the spirit. In one class Lorri and I had sit spots about a hundred yards apart. Between us lay a grove of cedars, pine and oak, with a lake to one side. Our task was to walk toward each other's sit areas. We had not been to each other's sit spots before so we had no idea where we were headed. That may sound easy but we were not simply to head toward each other, we were to meet each other at a half-way point as we were both blindfolded and walking silently toward one another. Still, we had both surrendered to the voice of our Inner Vision to guide us and we met.

Another significant teaching tool of Grandfather's was fire. In Philosophy 4 we learned how to bend fire. The first time I participated in this group exercise I had an open heart but a skeptical mind. How could one possibly bend fire? I knew that Uri Geller was supposed to be able to bend spoons with just his mind but figured that maybe it was smoke, mirrors and camera tricks. I had never heard of anyone or seen anyone accomplish such a thing. I have no memory or notes of my first experience of fire bending. I have since participated in countless group sits around a fire where we bent it this way and that or changed the color of the flames or raised or diminished them.

What would be the point of bending fire? First, it shows one that there is a real connection between intention, choice, passion and need. All four are necessary in order to accomplish this or anything else. Second, it demonstrates the power of group intention, choice, passion and need. Some groups I have been with seemed lackadaisical about the fire bending exercise and so the results weren't that great; other groups I have been with had tremendous energy and the fire bending was spectacular. Third, fire bending taught me the importance of having an open mind as to the way energy flows in the world; not just physical energy, but also Life Force and spiritual energy. When Lorri and I run workshops we have occasionally used fire bending. It is so fun to hear the "Wows" and see the awe when a group succeeds.

What is fire? It is energy. Wood or fuel, mixed with oxygen and a spark, produces a flame. That flame is energy being released. What is a thought in the brain? It is energy, a signal being transmitted from one synapse to another. You might say that is all true but thoughts remain in our heads while the fire remains outside of us. Maybe, if we lived in an atomistic world where everything had a discrete boundary, that would be true. We live, however, in a world that we now know can be described as a collection of fields or what is known in physics, in its simplest form, as Unified Field Theory. Everything is connected. All energy, whether of a distant star, the fire, or our thoughts are all forms of energy and they are all connected.

One hundred years ago, before Einstein published his studies on relativity this would have been unheard of but now, especially since the advent of quantum mechanics and string theory, our understanding of life at both the atomic and cosmic levels has changed. It is no longer a stretch, then, to say that it is possible for the human mind to interact with physical reality and change it. Accepting this as a possibility is the first step, getting there is a whole other thing.

This becomes especially true in the realm of prayer. In his discussion of the armor of God the biblical letter writer says that we are to "Offer prayers and petitions in the spirit at all times" (Eph 6:18. Some translations capitalize the word as Spirit. I wonder if this should be the case). Over the years I have had people share with me that they felt their prayers were ineffectual. I too have felt that many of my prayers went as far as the ceiling and then dropped back down to earth. I was never fond of the "Name it and Claim it" type of prayer, nor was I fond of all the books that proposed to give me the "secret of prayer." If it was secret, then it was Gnostic, thus special knowledge for special people, and I could not go in that direction. No, if our prayers were to really be prayers that wrought transformation then the power to do so should be available anywhere, anytime, to anyone.

As I mused over fire bending, power, field theory and prayer it occurred to me, that like all things spiritual, as long as I was praying for my own benefit, my prayers would never be heard. Since that time I have given up praying for myself, I leave that to others who love me. Today I only pray for others. If I find my prayers are caught up in ego or selfish ambition I know instantly that they have failed.

I have also discovered that prayer without passion produces empty words. I must truly desire what I am praying for in order for my prayer to be heard. For too long too many of my prayers were just wishes. I prayed wishing for this or that, hoping for this or that but never really wanting deeply for something good to happen to another. When I prayed for myself I could drum up lots of passion. I have since learned to find that same passion when seeking aid, comfort, healing, or enlightenment for others.

Grandfather said that prayers consisting only of words would never bring real change. He spoke of the need to visualize what it was we are praying for. I could not tell you how many times I have prayed The Lord's Prayer. In church services all over I still find that we pray that prayer without much passion, and we certainly don't take the time to visualize each petition. So for example, when I am talking to you about my wife, I visualize her or when I am describing a beautiful sunset from my recent trip to Australia, I visualize it. Take a moment and ask yourself, when was the last time you visualized the Lord's Prayer. We zoom past the opening words "Our Father" but do we take the time to see a real genuine loving nurturing parent smiling upon us or holding our hands? We say "hallowed be your name" without any real awareness of what that might mean and do not visualize God distinguishing God's self from all the gods of our fantasy, imagination and idolatry. "Thy Kingdom come?" When is the last time we stopped to imagine what the reign of God looks like in real life? Or of God feeding us? Or of those we have hurt and who have really hurt us? Have we visualized saying words of forgiveness to them, of being reconciled? Need I say more?

To visualize is to give power to prayer. Words are vehicles; they can be empty or full depending on how much we empower them. We know this best when we are really angry at someone; our words are loaded with emotion and passion. We say "we can't see straight" when we are mad. We spend time envisioning conversations and debates with others in our heads and how we are going to get them the next time we speak to them. When we do this we are visualizing or empowering these negative situations. In the same manner, we can visualize or empower positive dynamics in life. These dynamics, when they reflect the character of the Creator and Reconciler of the Universe, become reality because they are oriented to life, light, love, healing, reconciliation, peace, joy, or in short the fruits of the Holy Spirit the apostle Paul mentions in his letter to the Galatians.

One of the most helpful exercises in this regard that Tom taught us was "tree preaching." Some preachers take pride in being able to say they have preached in churches around the world. I enjoy preaching as much as the next person, but I think my best sermons have come to congregations of oaks, maples, cedars, hemlocks and pines. I love tree preaching, it has always been cathartic for me. Tree preaching is simply praying out loud to the Creator in the presence of the creation. Depending on where I am, I usually "preach" in a quiet whisper. But I preach with passion! I pour my heart out to the trees.

They can be pretty Stoic though. I enjoy Pentecostal audiences and their affirmations. Once I'm warmed up however, I have always felt like the trees listened with great attention. It's as if I can see what I am saying. When I tree preach I visualize the meaning of my words.

When I first heard Peter Jackson intended to make a movie of the Lord of the Rings I was quite nervous. Could he really bring Gandalf, Frodo and Elrond to life as I imagined them? Or the orcs, or the dwarves or the ents? Tolkien's ability to create landscapes made me wonder how Jackson would envisage the Shire or Moria, Rivendell, Lothlorien or Mordor. As a child I had used my imagination to fill in Tolkien's descriptions of Middle Earth. I'm glad to say I wasn't disappointed.

In the same way I pray now by seeing what I am saying. I envision my petitions. If I ask for a healing I see the person healed; if I ask for enlightenment, I see the person having an "Aha" moment. I like to think that this was what made Jesus' prayers so effective. He had a great imagination, seeing the possibilities of a world where God reigned in love, peace and justice. He envisaged that world and then went about using his power to make it a reality in the lives of those he met.

In the same way, spiritual warfare requires more than words. It demands a vision of what will be changed. When I read the writings of Dr. Martin Luther King Jr., I am amazed at the visualization he uses. His ability to evoke the imagination through the use of biblical metaphors and stories is remarkable. I think this is part of what made his work so powerful. He was able to see a new world, a world in which people treated each other as equals, a world where peace and justice kissed and where no person was left without their daily bread.

I recall when I was about twenty years old, Lorri and I went to visit George Eldon Ladd who had just retired as Professor of New Testament at Fuller Theological Seminary. George asked me what I wanted to do with my life and I shared with him my excitement about becoming a theologian. "Theology", he muttered. "Well, if you are going to study theology, you might as well first learn to eat sawdust without butter." He saw theology as boring, dry, and stuffy. He was right. A lot of theology is just that. Then there are those theologians who are able to take the dead bones of theological words and animate them through the use of story that forces the imagination to picture life, God and the world in a new way. Martin Luther was one, Karl Barth another. My goal has been to be such a theologian, one who inspired imagination and passion.

Evil resents imagination. The lifeblood of evil is fear which renders one powerless and keeps one frozen in a cage. Imagination or visualization is the opposite of fear. When we visualize a healing or reconciliation we set in motion that energy which will bring it to pass in the physical world. When our prayers are visualized, when our words become pictures, they become works of art that make things happen. "Please God, make it happen" prayers just don't work. Envisioning what we desire that is good and beneficial for another works. There is no secret to prayer, it is just a matter of being a little child and once again seeing what it is we desire that would benefit the other. Our insight and imagination is the flame that lights the fire of genuine change.

Chapter 11
Tom Brown and Angels

October and November passed quickly and my mind was reeling from all I had experienced in Philosophy 1-4. I had had more than enough and needed time to practice and weave all of these new experiences into my life. More than that, I could not process them fast enough. It seemed as if every day brought a paradigm shift. I remember feeling all of joint, as though I was being stretched and pulled in every new direction. My mind had somehow found itself inside a taffy machine and was being twisted this way and that. It was a good thing then that I had caught up with Lorri and we could be partners in Philosophy 5, 6 and 7. I needed someone to debrief with on an hourly basis and she has always been a great listener and advisor. She had three years to process her experiences of Philosophy 1-4. I had two weeks.

I was *slowly* getting what she meant when she had returned home from Philosophy 4 in the fall of 2002 and said she finally understood Jesus. Thanksgiving that year, as I recall, was an oasis following Philosophy 4. I can't say I followed my beloved New York Giants football season as closely as I wanted that fall. I am sure my friends thought I had gone off the deep end. At work my nickname "Dancing with Squirrels" started making a more regular appearance. When I was asked what I was doing in these classes I had no way to reply. I would mutter something about learning about Native ways and turn the conversation elsewhere. Fortunately two of our daughters had also taken some classes so, in our family, we had many discussions about our experiences.

Philosophy 5 and 6 were held in December. The cold presented a new challenge, that of distraction. Time and again I had to be aware when I allowed myself to feel sorry for myself as I sat there outside in my sit spot freezing my tush off so I could instead focus on what I was to be doing. My sit spot in Philosophy 3 and 4 was a berm with a swamp on one side and a small creek flowing straight away from me which I faced. I have used that same spot since then in other classes. I just love it. My partner in Philosophy 2 was a lieutenant in Naval Intelligence who used it as his sit spot in a previous class and showed it to me. Thanks LT! What is strange to me is that when I used this sit spot the Doobie Brothers song *Black Water* insisted on playing in my head. At first that drove me nuts and made meditation difficult, now I just change the station to George Winston or Kitaro.

Sit spots are another tool Grandfather used to teach a myriad of lessons to Tom and Rick. I don't use sit spots as much as I desire or should but from time to time find myself needing to "go sit." In a sit spot one not only discovers the baseline of the natural world but also how the natural world changes from day to day, week to week, month to month and season to season. If you are fortunate enough to live near a wooded area having a regular sit in your sit spot for thirty minutes a day will change your life. When you sit, you can simply pay attention to the natural world or you may choose to surrender to the presence of the area. You might take a walk in your "inner wilderness" through the use of the long form meditation mentioned earlier. With your eyes open you superimpose your interior wilderness picture on the exterior wilderness you see with your physical eyes. Often I will sit in quiet and then pray and then sit in the quiet again. We are only limited by our imaginations as we see leaves turning color, listen to the birdsongs, feel the wind inhale and exhale or feel the rain wash us clean or the sun warm our bodies. As far as I can recall there is not a class, except the Standard class where we did not use sit spots.

At first I didn't enjoy my sits, I found my mind wandering and I became easily bored. Over time I have come to delight in them, knowing that the first exercise each morning of class will involve something to do with my sit area. I think of that berm by the creek as one of the best friends and teachers I have ever known.

Philosophy 5 and 6 were, in many ways, expansions on Philosophy 3 and 4. We did a lot of presence exercises and some fire bending, we visited the sacred areas in the Primitive Camp and engaged in spiritual warfare. My groups in Philosophy 3 and 4 were exceptional. The classes felt in sync and the commitment of those present seemed apparent. I recall Tom being quite pleased with how those classes went. In Philosophy 5 I would face a new challenge, a new distraction: idiots. Sometimes students come to class, it can be any class, and they are just there to bide the time or get a certificate or say I reached such and such a level. Their commitment to the study and practice of whatever the teacher is passing on is minimal. They make trouble for others. In my notebook for Philosophy 5 I had written, "Idiots in class." This was on that first Monday morning. Apparently they wasted no time in bothering me or else I was being hypersensitive.

In 2011 I took a ten day class and on the 5th day drove home. I was pissed off at the way certain students were behaving. I left Lorri there to finish; she is much more patient than I am. After talking with my friend Jonathan I did turn around that next day and drive back but I did so with a great deal of irritation. I work well in groups where others really want to learn; I don't seem to tolerate fools very easily. Philosophy 5 was my entry into learning how to set aside my ego; and the Apprentice class of 2011 was the last time I allowed other students to affect my learning curve. Now I attend a class having no expectations of others. If some want to be idiots I let them, that is their business. I am there to learn everything I can. In the most recent class I have taken, in January 2013, the group I was part of was fantastic and the class was incredibly cohesive.

Sometimes Tom gets to me. How can I describe Tom? Words like aloof, elitist, introvert or commanding easily spring to mind but they are not really accurate. They most likely tell you more about me than Tom. Until 2011 in the Philosophy 9 class I had always felt inadequate around Tom. After all these years and all of the classes I have taken I am not even sure he knows my name. That used to really bother me. His constant hyperbole annoyed me as did the way I felt he could be pompous. If you go online and Google Tom Brown Jr., you will find others who have had similar opinions and who have walked away from the school after a few classes. I pity them. Once you get around his gruff exterior he really is a teddy bear.

Tom is no angel and he would be the first to admit it. Like all of us he has to face his personal demons on a daily basis. He has had a difficult time keeping instructors and managing the school. Yet, for all of his warts and flaws there is a genuine core to the man that I have come to like, even love. I suppose I am a lot like Tom and that is why I see him the way I do. Now I am just grateful to sit, listen, learn, absorb and know I am learning from a Grand Master. I often tell people that Tom's classes are the best pedagogical bang for the buck I have ever spent. They are the only classes where I can go back to my notebooks, full of exercises and practice over and over again and think through in new and different ways all I have learned.

What drives Tom is his passion to share Grandfather's vision. It must be lonely as there is only Tom left as the link in the chain back to

Grandfather. I wonder if some of the apostles felt the same way. Perhaps the last apostle alive, maybe the writer of the Fourth Gospel (the Gospel of John) felt it. Tom brings his passion to every class and that passion is what drives the class to excellence. Like Jesus with his passion for God's reign of peace, justice and joy, Tom's passion fuels every exercise and peppers every lecture. Sometimes students don't understand this and it inhibits Tom from taking the whole class where he had hoped; most times, though, it is catching. Philosophy 5 and the Apprentice classes were the two anomalies I experienced. I understand Tom's passion; for I think I have a similar passion for the gospel as Tom does for what he learned from Grandfather; and I appreciate that.

Tom met Grandfather when he was just eight years old and would spend almost every waking moment he was not in school with his friend Rick (Grandfather's blood grandson) learning from Grandfather until he was eighteen years old and Grandfather headed back to his native land in northern Mexico to die. Tom tells his story in a number of books; the one which made him famous is *The Tracker*. He also tells Grandfather's story or at least some interesting parts of it in *Grandfather* which was the first book I read walking around Central Park.

Tom has all together written some seventeen books. They come in two types: wilderness survival guides and philosophy. A reader wishing to explore more about what I have written about may wish to read *Grandfather*, *Awakening Spirits*, and *The Journey*. I have read and reread many of his books and each time I see things I had not seen before.

I would not want to give you the wrong impression of Tom. The vast majority of his students love him dearly. So much so that at the end of one of my Philosophy classes, during the Christmas season, someone wrote:

"You better watch out, you better not spy

You better not snivel, I'm telling you why

Santa Claus is really Tom Brown.

He's making a list, he's checking it twice

If you want to learn more, go ask the friggin' mice

Cuz Santa Claus is really Tom Brown.

He knows when you've been sleeping

He knows when you've been baked

He knows if you've had sex or not

So you better not masturbate, Oooohhh

You better watch out, you better not spy

You better not snivel, I'm telling you why

Santa Claus is really Tom Brown."

Silliness can sometimes take over at Tracker classes, but it's all good.

By the time Philosophy 5 rolled around the skeptic in me had given way to the experimenter. I didn't take Tom's word for anything but had to go prove it for myself. Sometimes I would repeat an exercise for myself, other times I would practice with Lorri and still other times I would teach it to others to see if they also had similar results. I needed to make sure that this wasn't all just in my head. Lorri and I would run seminars, retreats and conferences where we taught what we had learned. My real interest was to see replicable results. Some folks balked when we mixed bible study and theology with these skills, but most found them to be energizing and life-giving.

We practiced a lot of healing in the Philosophy classes. There are many ways to heal, many of them are quite rudimentary, and I found some to be frustrating and others to be easy. The stories of Grandfather as a healer resonated with my knowledge of Jesus and the apostolic church as healers. My greatest concern was still that we were dabbling in new age idiocy. I have heard enough charlatans to know that healers aren't all they are cracked up to be; and I didn't want to end up sounding like I had just come from some mental institution and could hear voices. Nor did I want to engage in practices that I felt were suspect. Healers that charged money to "move energy" really irked me. The power of suggestion can be great, and while I am sure there are honest healers out there and that some folks have truly been helped, I have always felt there is just a lot of bullshit as well. I had invested too much of my life becoming a critical thinker to simply believe that one could lay hands on someone, move a little energy and all would be well. That's $150, thank you very much.

As I said it may be that Tom Brown is no angel, but because of him I have had to change my mind about the angelic. My friend of blessed memory, Walter Wink, wrote a great deal about angels. He did not mean angels in the sense of supernatural beings that could descend with wings and battle evil like so many Hollywood movies depict them. When Walter spoke of angels he was referring to the angel of a group or its corporate expression as a personality. Groups have their own character as do corporations or institutions. The corporate personality of a group is its angel. Walter found this in the book of

Revelation where the prophet John writes letters to seven churches but addresses, not the communities, but the "angels of the churches."

In Philosophy 2 we had dealt a little bit with "good spirits" or guardian spirits. Belief in angels is a bit tricky. One can be a literalist and end up with a mixed bag of biblical-medieval-Hollywood angels or one can go to the other extreme saying that they are relics of a bygone mythical religious superstition. The great Swiss theologian Karl Barth devoted a section of his massive *Church Dogmatics* to angels and their mission and was taken to task by scholars who felt he had not demythologized his thinking.

I had entered Philosophy 2 as a dyed-in-the-wool skeptic. Angels and demons were outmoded ways of talking about good and evil. People who had claimed to have seen angels needed to get treatment, I supposed. I had never seen an angel. Either they were very, very good at hiding themselves (which I did not suppose) or many people were suffering acid flashbacks (which I wondered about having grown up in San Francisco). Either way, I thought all of this talk about guardian spirits was just nonsense. Even when I "met" my guardian angels in a meditation I chalked it up to a form of psychological projection although the character of my angels gave me pause. I had "met" four of them: some kind of wandering Cynic, an African-American 19th century herbalist grandmother, a mute Native scout and a little girl who suffered with physical deformities. Not exactly whom I would pick for guardian angels!

Having read Walter's work on corporate spirits had the effect of keeping my mind open to the possibility that the exercises we would do to discern them had some merit. Our group gathered at our group area where we had built a fire. As a group we all projected our need for the group "angel" to come forth. Our goal was not see anything but to feel or sense the group spirit and all of us would write down what we discerned. Seven of the eight of us wrote "joyful" and "covering, tent or dome" while five of the eight of us wrote "protective warrior." I found this amount of congruence astonishing.

We might think in other terms in order to understand this phenomenon. We use language like school spirit or a mob spirit. This "spirit" is the corporate angel of the group and if change is to be affected it is this angel that must be addressed. Whenever I enter a room with many people or a lecture hall, classroom, church or gathering, I like to surrender and see what I can discern about the group spirit. This often helps me particularly when I am teaching or preaching. I want my message to be heard; so I try to address the group angel. I don't know of any study that has been done on this but someone should someday analyze the speeches and sermons of Dr. King to see how his words addressed a corporate "angel" or structural power.

Philosophy 6 was a greater expansion of Philosophy 5. The difficulty I have in writing about Philosophy 6 is that so much material we covered concerns exercises, concepts and experiences I have not previously recorded in these pages and introducing them at this point would just muddy the waters. Suffice it to say that after Philosophy 6, I was ready for the Christmas break. I had just been through six of the most intense, strangest weeks of my life and needed a 'time-out' in the worst way. I especially needed time to get over my skepticism which came roaring back as soon as I arrived home. I wanted to just label everything as psychological projection or group hypnosis. On the other hand there was just too much evidence that something else had occurred, that there was another aspect of reality I had not noticed for forty-eight years of my life.

I only had three weeks to sit with what I had learned. Philosophy 7 was just around the corner. Once again I was not prepared for what was to come.

Chapter 12

Pull the Pin But Don't Drop the Grenade

Unlike Philosophy 1-6, Philosophy 7 was held somewhere near Fort Myers, Florida. Oh beautiful warm weather! Lorri and I had driven down with all our camping gear. The car was jammed. Straight through we went but after twenty hours of driving from Long Island, sometime around 4 am when neither of us could continue any further. We were falling asleep so we stopped at a motel to rest. Later that day we completed our trip.

The class was held at a scout camp of some sort. The weather was perfect. We pitched our tents and got ready for the usual Sunday night preparations. Monday morning dawned clear, bright and warm. Coffee somehow tastes better when it is cold outside but I have never passed it up, so I made my way to the lecture/dining hall to get some morning joe. This was the first time Tom had ever run a Philosophy 7 class and the excitement level among the students was very high. As I recall we were close to eighty students that week.

If there was a theme to Philosophy 7 that year one might call it communication. We had done all sorts of work in previous classes learning how to hear our Inner Vision, to communicate with one another through sending and receiving, sensing presence and various other means. This class would take communication to a whole new level.

Since so many of our exercises take place outside and we are spread out all over the landscape, the School utilizes a system of call-outs when an exercise is complete and we are to return to the main building. Someone yells "Come on in" and it is repeated by everyone who hears it so that it is echoed scores of times so that the farthest person knows it is time to come in. I was therefore, completely surprised when Tom announced that this class would not use call-ins. How were we supposed to know when our sit spot or group exercise was finished? Tom indicated that he would send out a call "mentally." Oh, sure. I could just see it. I would be out in my sit spot waiting and waiting and waiting; and for some reason my internal 'call waiting' would be disabled; and I was going to be the one to not hear the call in. The first time we were sent to our sit spots for an exercise I was in a complete panic. How was I supposed to focus on what I was to do and listen for 'call waiting' at the same time? I don't know how, but it all worked out in the end. At the right time I felt like it was time to go in; and as I came closer I saw students coming from all directions to the main building. Beam me up Scotty! The damned thing worked.

In another exercise Lorri and I sat across from each other with several sticks lined up between us. One of us would send to the other a "mental communication" as to which stick to pick up. We managed to hit it spot on seven out of eight times. This is not as easy as it sounds and I was relieved that we were able to do it at all. I initially thought it was a matter of luck; but as we did it over and over again I began to wonder about the odds. What were they? Out of eight times, what could the odds be that we could get seven correct decisions as to which stick our partner was "asking" us to choose? 1% or less I supposed. Something else was happening here, something I couldn't put my finger on, something that was greater than my mind could comprehend.

You have all heard of *The Horse Whisperer* and there is that fellow on television that somehow seems to be able to communicate with the worst behaved dogs and turn them into well behaved animals.

Then there is Dr. Doolittle who could talk to the animals. I can't say that I have ever had a really good conversation with an animal. Seriously, is it possible to have a serious conversation with a species that cleans their privates with their tongue? I don't think so. So when Tom asked us to go listen to the plants I knew it was time for me to check out.

Lorri has some books at home on how plants respond to human language and music. There is also the interesting research of Masaru Emoto on how human emotions affect the environment. Emoto has some fascinating photography of water molecules and how they are really quite dramatically affected by human emotion directed at them. I was quite prepared to go out to the bush and talk to the plants, there is a lot I could say. Whether they could hear or not didn't matter to me. We were not to talk to the plants, however, we were to listen to them speak to us. By this time I had become a sucker who would try anything once. So off I went to do the exercise.

I was to find a plant that I had no knowledge of or did not recognize at all. No problem as I have never really excelled at plant identification. At some point I found a likely candidate. It was a large overgrown shrub type thing with leaves. I guessed that qualified as a plant. The next step was a specific form of communing and listening carefully to the question we would ask the plant. I set my phaser to stun just in case and opened my communication device. "What are your medicinal properties" I asked. Remember the old television sets from the 1950's and how when you turned them on at first there was this little dot that appeared in the middle of the screen? Then how slowly a picture would emerge? Something like that happened. I saw a pair of shins; I have no idea whose shins, with varicose veins, then the image faded away. What in the world could this mean?

The next step in the process was to take our 'discovery' back to the main room where there were scores of field guides, find our plant and look up either the folkloric or pharmacological evidence of the medicinal properties of the plant. I searched and searched the field guides but could not locate my plant. Everybody else seemed to be able to find theirs, but not me. Finally I went to one of the instructors who I knew was really good at this plant thing, got on my knees and begged for help. Off we went to go look at the plant I had chosen. The instructor laughed out loud. Of course I couldn't find my plant in the North American field guides; this was a plant from South America. It happened to be a Brazilian pepper plant and the capsaicin from its seed pods was beneficial for things like leg vein problems.

There were several more exercises where we as partnerships would "communicate" telepathically. Lorri and I have found over the years that I am a better receiver and she is a very strong sender. I don't think this is quite fair, but like the apostle Paul says, we all have our gifts. We did an exercise where we were to sit facing one another with two sticks between us. One partner would "tell" the other to turn the sticks, like hands on a clock to a certain time. So, for example, I might have Lorri turn the pointed end of one stick to 2 o'clock and the second stick to 9 o'clock with mental commands. We seemed to do pretty well with this.

On another occasion we would practice "touching" one another mentally and then sense where our partner was touching us. I would like to say that I behaved myself in this exercise but that would be lying. It was too much fun. I should mention that I have only ever done this with Lorri, to do otherwise would surely be a one way ticket to the obsidian wall!

One of my favorite exercises has to do with finding a trailhead that lead down a trail we had never been on. We would then "walk" that trail in our "spirits", see what there was to see, note anything unusual, and then return to our body that stood there at the trailhead. We would then write down what we saw, share it with our partners and head out on the trail to confirm what we had seen. I couldn't believe it, this stuff really worked. There is a great Bud Light commercial where the football fans are awaiting a field goal and they turn their bottles so that the labels all face the same direction. One fellow fan wants to know what they are doing. Two guys give some sort of metaphysical explanation and finally the third fan turns and says, "It's like magic, only real." That is how I began to feel about the stuff I was learning. Who needed Hogwarts and Dumbledore when there was The Tracker School and Tom Brown?

If energy can be felt or discerned and manipulated it can also be taken and transformed. By Thursday afternoon and dozens of new exercises under our belts we were ready to really have some fun. We spent some time that afternoon in our partnerships taking and giving energy to our partners. First we would drain a little energy, and then we would give back that energy plus some. We were to do this at least three times to each other, alternating back and forth. We were warned that "by the end you may feel confused and you might think you can only feel through your ass." I thought this was more hyperbole. It wasn't. When I got home I practiced this with my youngest granddaughter, Laurelin. Ever since she had been born it had become my task (and gift) to put her down for a nap. Now that she was five years old and I was at the place where I needed a nap, we would lay down on my bed and start the "Quiet honey, Grandpa is trying to sleep" talk which as some of you know can go on for a long time as five year olds seem to ask a lot of questions at nap time. When we returned from this class, and nap time came, I gave her a little kiss on the forehead, told her I loved her, held her hand and drained a little energy. She fell fast asleep. I only did this four or five times just to prove to myself that it worked and soon we were back to the "Quiet honey, Grandpa is trying to sleep" talk. Eventually she no longer took naps; but I am stuck in a rut and need my daily nap.

Like the other Philosophy classes we did a lot of healing work. Now there are times when someone is of two minds about being healed or they have an emotional investment in being sick. Perhaps being sick brings them attention or something. Not everyone wants to be healed. The Gospels record that Jesus couldn't heal all of the people all of the time and the people's faith played a role in their healing. Sometimes it is necessary to break down a wall or indecision in a patient's mind, to help them see that they really do want to be healed in spite of what they may say.

This next exercise was powerful but had potentially dangerous consequences. Our groups of eight were scattered about the landscape, all within calling distance of the main dining hall where Tom and the instructors would be. Our group formed a circle on a vast expanse of lawn. Seven of us would be on the outside and one of us would be "the patient" in the middle. Our task was similar to draining energy, only this time the group would drain the mind of the patient. That is, they would remove their thoughts. After a count of twenty or so, the group would return the thoughts. One group member was to act as a lifeguard to start and stop us and keep an eye on the person in the middle. If we ran into any kind of distress or anything we could not handle the lifeguard would yell out and Tom would come to our aid. We had our *deus ex machina*. Tom was very clear that this exercise was like handing a two-year old a hand grenade. He said "Pull the pin, but don't let go of the grenade."

So we gathered in our circle and each member took turns being a lifeguard and the patient. Every person who would "come out" from under, as it were, had the same tale: They were thinking; then something happened; then here they were again. For some it was like coming out of anesthesia. The skeptic in me was certain that we had been seduced by some sort of hypnotic suggestion. How could it be possible for someone to remove another person's thoughts? Really now! So I came up with a fool proof plan to show that this was actually impossible.

When it was my turn to be the 'patient', I had decided to recite the lyrics to a song I like. These lyrics are quite complex and strange. The song was *The Revealing Science of God* by *Jon Anderson and Yes*. The lyrics open like this:

> "Dawn of light lying between A silence and sold sources Chased amid fusions of wonder In moments hardly seen forgotten Colored in pastures of chance Dancing leaves cast spells of challenge Amused but real in thought We fled from the sea whole Dawn of thought transferred through moments Of days under searching earth Revealing corridors of time provoking memories Disjointed but with purpose Craving penetrations offer links With the self instructors sharp And tender love as we took to the air A picture of distance…"

You get the picture. This goes on and on and I have known it by heart since I was fifteen years old. I figured if I lay there and starting singing the song in my mind, it would force me to focus as these are lyrics easy to mess up. When I focus I always get them right. By being focused I could prevent the group from removing my thoughts. In my mind I began reciting,

"Dawn of light lying between A silence and sold sources Chased amid fusions of wonder In moments hardly seen forgotten

C   o   l

         o   r

           e   d

When I came to there was my group smiling at me asking how I was and was I ready to debrief. Debrief what, I wondered? What was I doing lying on the ground? It took me a few minutes to get my bearings. From that point on I was convinced, and the skeptic decided to take a little holiday.

There were many other things we learned about in Philosophy 7 that surpassed my wildest imagination. For imagination it had become. The capacity to imagine a world where light shone in the darkness, where healing disease was the norm not the exception, where love trumped hate, prejudice and discrimination, where forgiveness ended violence and where the lion lay down with the lamb. I imagined all of us as human healers, which I think was Tom's goal and Grandfather's vision; it was certainly Jesus' vision. Everything we learned had as its goal to teach us how to heal one another and how to heal our Mother the Earth.

I had managed to go through Philosophy 1-7 all in a row but it would be another four years before Tom would offer Philosophy 8. I would need all four of those years to just begin to integrate all I had learned and to practice, practice, practice. Later that year we moved from Long Island to Lancaster, PA. Our lives shifted from the crazy, insane dog-eat-dog lifestyle of New York to the more pastoral and rural ways of life among the Amish and the Mennonites. We camped more often, took nature walks more often and generally grew to appreciate all we had learned. We would begin our non-profit Preaching Peace (**www.preachingpeace.org**), and I would publish my first book during that time (*Stricken by God?* co-edited with my friend Brad Jersak). Things were blooming in our lives and we were finally living our dream.

Chapter 13

The Coming Darkness?

After 9/11 it felt like everybody and their brother had a doomsday scenario. The best selling book of all time, actually a series of books titled *Left Behind*, was pseudo-speculative theological bullshit, Fundamentalist Dispensational nonsense. Not that I have an axe to grind or anything, but I detest the fact that so many people worldwide read this Christian trash and think that it is the Bible truth, God's very Word. It just gets my blood boiling. I would be very tempted to think every copy of that book out of existence but that would be going to the dark side. Crazy irony, isn't it?

It is true that there exists what scholars call an apocalyptic element in the New Testament. Some scholars in the (in)famous Jesus Seminar thought that all the apocalyptic stuff in Jesus' teaching was added later by the church. In other words, all the end of the world, universe falling apart stuff was not part of Jesus' message but was part of the Jewish worldview of the early Christians. I'm not quite as convinced as some scholars, but refuse to believe that things are as they are portrayed in the *Left Behind* books.

Certain types of Fundamentalist Christians have proposed a theory whereby God breaks history down into various periods of time, known as dispensations. There are seven such dispensations beginning in the year the universe was created "6,000 years ago." Right! We are now allegedly in the next to last dispensation. Soon The Rapture will happen taking all the good little Christian boys and girls to heaven and leaving the rest of the sinful godless world to face the Great Tribulation. There is a supposed timeline about when this is going to occur based upon fulfillment of certain prophecies.

I think it is fair to say that I don't hold to any of this. Ever since the second century, Christian prophets have been announcing the end of the world. Montanus thought the New Jerusalem would descend around the year 170. At the turn of the first millennium, Christian prophets announced the end of the world; and at the time of the Reformation, Martin Luther was certain he was living in the last days. It seems that every age thinks that it will be the last to walk God's green earth.

On the other hand scientists who plot the doomsday clock have it at four minutes to midnight. That gives me pause. Problems attendant upon climate change and some proposed terrible scenarios by scientists ring all too true. More than that however, one of my significant mentors, René Girard, who taught at Stanford University and is a member of the French Academy wrote a book a few years ago called *Battling to the End* in which he argued that humanity is heading for a time of all out violence if it does not repent of its destructive ways. I am between a rock and a hard place when it comes to figuring out just what *kind* of time we are living in.

I was not caught completely off guard when in March of 2008 Lorri and I joined the Philosophy 8 class and found that Tom was in an apocalyptic frame of mind. He spoke a lot in that class about the coming darkness based upon a series of prophecies in which

Grandfather had been given dreams and visions. The thing that bothered me most is that Tom had a timeline for when certain things were going to happen, it reminded me of the Christian Fundamentalist Dispensational timeline.

For me, timelines seem to be oriented to a sort of fatalism or determinism. It is as if there is no way out once you pronounce a timeline. I remember last year when a well known TV preacher announced the end of the world in May and then, when that didn't happen, readjusted it to October. Of course that didn't happen either. Then a few months later there was supposed to be the Mayan apocalypse of December 21, 2012. That didn't happen. Here I am in 2013 writing this book when the world should have fallen apart several times over.

When people talk about the end of the world is it possible they are just taking their own life and projecting it onto the global picture? All of our lives end and I have already mentioned how we both live in fear of death and denial of it at the same time. We just don't seem to know how to come to terms with the end of our lives. I don't wish to deny that the world *feels* like it is falling apart. 9/11 sent shock waves throughout all of us, subsequent wars and rumors of wars, saber-rattling by nations like North Korea and Syria, genocidal massacres in Africa, the increase of domestic violence including serial killings in malls, theaters and schools unhinges me as much as it does anyone else. Add to that the increase in superbugs, climate change, super-storms and the like and life does have an apocalyptic feel to it. But is there a timeline? That was bothering me. Since I couldn't figure out whether or not the end of the world was coming I decided to just focus on today. Martin Luther was once asked if the end of the world was coming tomorrow what he would do. He replied he would plant a tree. Focusing on the present was either an act of denial or an act of hope, but it worked for me.

The apostle Paul says that there comes a time in a person's life where they put away childish things and become mature adults. My entry into recovery was like this. There I learned to put away self-destructive habits, take responsibility for my life, learned how to feel feelings and how to have real relationships. Being a theologian has been like this as well. My search for Truth with a capital T gave way to a deep Skepticism which in turn has morphed into Ricoeur's 'second naïveté' where I still quest for genuine truth but accept that it is not about the destination but about the road traveled.

I was to find that Philosophy 8 was to be a class where all we had previously learned would be put away and a new level of maturity would develop. All of the "tricks", techniques, signs, symbols and other devices we had learned to help us on the way were transcended. They were crutches that got us all started out walking but would need to be discarded. Grandfather told Tom and Rick a story, a parable, about the need to transcend what he called the "hairs" of religion. This is my very brief paraphrase of it: A man ends up with a genie. The genie would grant the man's wishes. The man wished for a house. The genie went out and built the house. He asked for a boat. The genie went and built a boat. He asked for many other things and each time the genie would build them for him faster and faster. Each time the genie returned he was larger and larger and more demanding as to what the next wish would be. After a while the genie was huge and ferocious. The man was fast running out of things to occupy the genie. He was beside himself and so asked his neighbor, a wise sage what he could do to stop the genie from becoming larger and quicker. The man told him to give the genie a hair from his beard and ask the genie to straighten it out. The man went back, plucked a hair from his beard, and gave it to the genie with the instruction to straighten it. Each time the genie would try to straighten the hair it would spring back into its curly shape. Each time the genie did this it would grow smaller and meeker until finally the genie was so small and so quiet he no longer disturbed the man.[3]

Many times during a meditation or when learning a philosophy skill, we would find our minds and thoughts had become the enemy. When we were supposed to be feeling or sensing something I would often find my mind needing to jump in, like the genie. So we learned the value of giving our genie minds a hair to straighten so we could focus our attention on learning. All religions or spiritualities have a genie and need "hairs" in order to quiet the mind so that the self can go deeper into the spiritual or mystical side of reality. For Christians, hairs take the form of rituals or icons, certain types of singing or worship, or certain ways of reading and understanding the Bible. When we attend a church service we can often find ourselves preoccupied with these things. When I was a pastor, I tried to change some of the physical structure of the church as well as the ideas that people believed in. When I did I ran into huge trouble. People believe that the hairs are the point of Christian existence. They could not

---

[3] The full tale is told in the book *Awakening Spirits*, 56-60 by Tom Brown Jr.

see that their minds were preoccupied with those things which should have distracted their internal genie. Rather they had become the genie and could focus only on the 'hair.'

'Hairs' are useful tools for keeping the logical mind at bay; they are not the things in themselves that we were meant to focus our attention upon when we contemplated the mystery of the Divine. In order to really listen so that the "still small voice" can be heard it is necessary to purify our Inner Vision or that place where we can hear God speak to us. Our tendency is to only hear what we want God to say. When we do that we have turned God into an extension of our selves and created an idol. This is the problem of certainty in some expressions of religion. The need for intellectual certainty can manifest itself in both the totalitarian stance of the religious Fundamentalist and as the 'certainty of the uncertain' of the religious Progressive. When we are certain we are certain we leave no room for God to come in and change or transform us. We can so invest ourselves in forms of certitude that we end up stuck in a rut.

Philosophy 8 was like Ricoeur's second naïveté; we needed to move beyond the apparent techniques and move to a more mature interior sense of the truth. For me that will always be "the truth as it is in Jesus" (Eph. 4:21). Some may say my focus on Jesus is a hair; I would prefer to say it is a life long commitment to learning how to be fully human and connected with God as Jesus was fully human and connected with God. Christian spirituality is not a set of correct dogmas or doctrines; it is a path, a journey, a road to wholeness. Not for nothing is Jesus called "The Way" (John 14:6) or the first Christians followers of "the Way" (Acts 19:23). We can either be in a rut or in a groove. In a rut we get stuck and movement has ceased; in a groove we are constantly moving ahead. When we focus on the "hairs" of our religion and the need for certainty we find ourselves stuck in a rut. The only way to move from a rut to a groove is to transcend the hairs that fix our attention.

In addition to transcending hairs we learned a lot about the depth and sincerity of our passion for learning. Exercise after exercise challenged our passion. Did we really expect to see the results that were possible, or had our minds with their million gazillion questions stifled our passion? Once when Tom complained to Grandfather about the poor results he was having Grandfather said, "Apparently, grandson, what you are telling me is you didn't want it bad enough." So it was as Lorri and I would engage in some exercise, I would find myself not getting where I thought I should be.

Maybe this was more advanced than I could master, perhaps it was possible only for a select few. My mind would make excuses and I would believe them. Little wonder then that I found frustration mounting. I searched deep within myself and there at the center of my heart was The Skeptic sitting comfortably and all knowing. "Do you really believe all this nonsense?" it said, "Look at you, you fool. You have been sucked into this new age nonsense after all." I tried reasoning with The Skeptic. I had worked hard to make sense of this in terms of my theological research, my work in Girard's mimetic theory, disciplines like quantum theology, and my studies of Jesus, the four Gospels and the early church. Why wouldn't The Skeptic believe me? One could make sense of it if one tried. The Skeptic would not be quiet. It plied my soul with question after question and doubt after doubt. I was firmly in its grip.

It was then I recalled the Tunnel of Love from Philosophy 1 so many years before. In my heart I went back to that memory and recalled the overwhelming feeling of being loved and how deep and rich that love felt. I thought of how much my wife loved me in spite of all the terrible things I had done to her. I thought about the love of my daughters and granddaughters. Love was real. Love could not be denied. I defied The Skeptic to tell me that I wasn't loved or that I had not experienced Love in my deepest self, That God loved me with a deeper passion than I could begin to describe. Suddenly The Skeptic went silent. Love cannot be denied. The Skeptic suddenly realized that it too was loved, for The Skeptic was me and I was The Skeptic. From that point on 'The Skeptic' became 'the skeptic.' From now on, the skeptic would be critical thinking that assisted me. It no longer had the power to dominate me. Instead of being an enemy it would become my ally. That was a great moment.

Grandfather said that "faith is the most powerful force on earth." The Bible constantly talks about the importance of faith, not as assent to correct doctrine, but as an expression of trust, trust in the benevolence of God and God's mercies. The Skeptic, that relic from my childhood that would not, could not trust anything my mother said, had held me back from real faith. Little wonder that all my years of trying to follow Jesus were such a miserable failure. I had been listening to The Skeptic instead of trusting that I was unconditionally loved. Since then I have been learning to live a life of faith. I wake up and every morning is a new day where I experience God's great mercy, kindness and compassion. Whether my wife greets me with hug and a kiss, or a cardinal joins the sparrows by our birdfeeder or my daughter calls on the phone or my granddaughters come to play a game or I visit with my friend Jonathan, each of these is an experience not only of human love but of "Love Divine, All Loves Excelling." Instead of trying to find God in logical syllogisms, or doctrinal formulae, I am learning to listen to the Voice of Love that has come to me deep inside, the "Deep, Deep Love of Jesus."

Philosophy 8 was really about faith, faith that the Creator loves all creation, including me. Where I was once felt excluded from Love now I was embraced by it. Faith in that love gave me the courage to believe that just as God so loved the world, so I too could love the world. I could love those that didn't love me. I could love the Earth for her wondrous and gracious bounty. I could love my family. I believed this was possible and that possibility became my reality. Faith is not easy; trusting in love has not been easy. I need to remind myself each day that I am loved. All I need to do is open my eyes to see all of the tangible manifestations of love around me.

Only love can conquer darkness. It was love that conquered the darkness of my soul; it is God's love in Jesus that conquered the principalities and powers that bind humanity by exposing them as worthless frauds of death and destruction. On the last night of Philosophy 8 we made a journey back to Hell. Our exercise was to enter Hell with respect, but not to honor it or fear it. We were going to learn from it. We'd gathered in the darkness that had settled on the land and made our way down the firebreak to our group sit area in Hell. We had then dispersed to learn. We were to have an open heart and mind and to ask Hell a question. My question was "Why do you exist?"

I received as clear an answer as if a human voice had spoken in the darkness: "Because you made me. I exist to destroy humanity." In meditation, I could see a "face" appear in a tree twenty feet or so away from me. I began a conversation about fear with what I could only presume was an evil presence. I learned that the power of evil is fear and that people only believe in hell because they believe in their fears. The face at first had a kingly appearance but at some point shifted to a horrific countenance. "I own you," it said. My past sins had made me a slave to hell. I immediately denied that. "I am forgiven," I said, "You do not own me; I am freed from your bondage." My mind recalled the passage in the letter to the Hebrews that talked about Jesus overcoming the fear of death and how we too could lose fear's grip on our lives. I also recall reflecting that in the Light there is no fear. My notebook also records that I reflected upon the harrowing of Hell/Hades by Jesus between his death and resurrection.

My meditation continued when suddenly all of the area seemed to be encased in fog. The fog felt like ignorance or blindness, the blindness I had spent so much of my life dwelling within and that I sensed enveloped so much of humanity. Then the fog cleared and I found myself sitting under a huge arch. It had gates on either side that were completely broken and hanging off their hinges, like the ancient gates of a long abandoned city. I sensed that this was the entrance or portal to Hell. What struck me was how quiet Hell was. I pondered that for a moment then realized it was quiet because it was empty!

My perception shifted once again. I had grown so weary of this conversation. Hell's attempts to frighten me were not working. In the mist I saw myself surrounded by a waist high black wrought iron fence. Out in the darkness there was a human-like shadow making its way toward me. Its presence felt evil, in fact, it is the most evil presence I have ever felt. The presence was a total absence of light, it was cold and malevolent. Was that fear that I felt? Tom had once faced The Stalker of Hell, could this be the same figure? I refused to shudder. When it came yet closer still I commanded it to keep its distance. It stopped perhaps twenty feet away. I could see it clearly, about six feet tall and menacing. I asked its name. It refused. I commanded it to give me its name. It spoke its name and came closer. In front of me there began to materialize a light that turned into what I can only describe of as an angel with a flaming sword. I knew I was protected. Then as if a switch was turned, I was back in the physical world surrounded by my classmates and we began our journey back to the camp.

I have been to Hell since. There have been no overwhelming epiphanies; it has just been quiet for me. I have no fear of Hell or of death for Love has triumphed in my life. I cannot say what happened there that night but for me it was very real. I have faced the darkness in my soul many times. Tom has said that 90% of the darkness we will ever experience comes from within us. So it is that over the course of these Philosophy classes I have had to face my own demons and darkness and let the light of ultimate love overcome them.

I cannot say where the world is going. Perhaps we are headed for a time of apocalypse. It may be the case that we are headed for a time of great change. Tom may be interpreting Grandfather's prophecies correctly in which case I am glad to have learned how to become a child of the earth and can trust the Creator and the creation to take care of me should I ever need to leave civilization. Maybe he has read into Grandfather's prophecies his own concerns. It is not for me to say, things will come to pass either way. Wherever we are going I do not need to know if we are on a timeline out of my control; I just need to trust that love will endure. My own personal apocalypses where one reality ended and another began have all ended well. I believe that apocalypse is inevitable; I do not believe that apocalypse is bad. It simply means that a time for great change is upon us.

Hope is not wishful thinking; it is trust that in spite of all the evil we see and experience, Love will not let us go.

Chapter 14
Me, My Selves and I

My mother passed away on March 31, 2011. I spoke to her on the phone the night before she died. She had refused to take my call the day before. She had a tendency to withhold her love from us children as a way of punishing us. I supposed she was doing that at this time. My last words to her were "I love you, Mom." I could just barely feel them but I meant them sincerely. She had lived a broken life and had passed on her brokenness to me and my siblings; in turn I have passed that brokenness on to my own children. It is a generational thing of which we are all aware of on some level as we reflect on our parents and our own parenting. I have had a number of "conversations" with my mother since her death. Even though I wonder if she ever knew love while she lived I am certain that at the moment of her passing she experienced love as I had when I ventured into the Light in Philosophy 1. I used to hold her responsible for all of my failures and addictions; now I own them as my own. I have made peace with her memory thanks in large part to Grandfather's and Jesus' path.

Three years would pass between Philosophy 8 and Philosophy 9. Two weeks after my mother's death we would once again pack up to head to class. April 2011 was turning into a stunning springtime. Phil 9 would be held in the Primitive Camp so we could access the sacred areas more easily. These were the areas where Tom and Rick had learned their lessons so long ago. The Primitive Camp is a very special place to Tracker students. Grandfather's Camp is one of the most special places I have ever visited. It is not far from the outdoor classroom called "The Taj" where we learn under an outdoor canopy. Grandfather left Tom and Rick at age 93 in the late 1960's. Since then Tom and his students have cleared an area surrounding the place where Grandfather had his personal shelter. It has a fire pit in the center where time and again we have shared in exercises around a roaring fire. I recall one time when we were doing a meditation there and I suddenly found myself in the midst of a great party. There were all kinds of folks there and to my surprise there was Karl Barth and Dietrich Bonhoeffer! Surely this was a great place to be visiting.

Lorri and I pitched our tent, the big lovely tent we still use, not the three person pygmy tent. Mornings were cold, sometimes the temperature would drop near or below freezing but that no longer bothered me. I would waken and dress very quickly and make my way to a fire, have a cup of coffee and visit with fellow students until breakfast. The Philosophy 9 class was small, just under forty of us. There was an electric feel to the class; the excitement level was intense. Never before had Tom taught Phil 9, in fact of the eighty or so students who had attended the previous Phil 8 class, only about half of us were there for Phil 9.

That Monday we went on a "wander" to visit all of the sacred areas in the Primitive Camp: Prophecy Hill, Spirit Hill, Hell and Grandfather's Camp. Having been to each area time and again in both memory and hope, we built fire structures that we would use later in the week. That took the entire day and later that night we would enter Grandfather's camp and share in a special pipe ceremony in complete silence. The first day of each Philosophy class is a day of preparation but this felt different. It was as if the preparation was part of my own personal learning curve. No longer was the Day of Preparation a chore; now it felt essential and life-giving. It was while I was reflecting on that as I walked from place to place that I knew I had changed deep within. Perhaps it was my mother's passing, perhaps it was the new lease on life I felt from all the Philosophy classes or the feeling I had that God was using me again in answer to my prayers of so many years ago while getting stoned in the attic. Maybe it was all of the above and more. I didn't know and I didn't need to know why, it all just felt good.

Like most Christians I have my favorite portions of Scripture and sayings of Jesus. The opening prologue to The Gospel of John and the Sermon on the Mount are my two favorites. In the same way I have a favorite saying from Grandfather. "When you know that you know and you don't care how you know, then you've arrived." It took almost a decade of training before I would understand the power and wisdom of that saying; but as I wandered on that first day of Phil 9, I was walking on air.

On Tuesday morning Tom began his instruction on what Philosophy 9 was going to be all about. We were going to journey deep within. In the earlier Philosophy classes we had gone out from ourselves into the worlds of the Life Force and the spirit; this was different. The journey within meant that we would experience the sacredness within, as though we had walked into a Temple in our very soul. Since I have engaged in a lot of introspection I did not find this unusual. My Jungian phase in the 80's while I was in Seminary, my post-collapse healing phase of the 90's and my own personal recovery from addictions in the first decade of the 2000's have all been times of deep introspection.

I was a little taken aback when Tom said that while about 40% of Grandfather's teaching was on the realms of the Life Force and spirit, the remaining 60% had to do with the Temples of the Soul. After all these years it meant that I was just beginning to get to the real heart of the matter. I thought I had arrived only to find out that Philosophy 1-8 were just prolegomena to the real thing. Grandfather had said that "the way of the spirit is the testing ground to find out who is worthy to enter the Temples of the Soul." Tom described the difference between Philosophy 1-8 and Philosophy 9 as going from pre-school to med-school. I was certainly glad that The Skeptic had been tamed in Philosophy 8 or else I am sure I would never have had the extraordinary experiences I was about to have that week.

We spent the rest of Tuesday doing a number of exercises in our sit areas. I had chosen as my sit spot a place on a trail that paralleled the stream that ran through camp. At one spot the stream becomes a pond of sorts then tapers back to a stream. The current of the stream is rather brisk year-round but where it becomes a pond the current goes deep and the surface of the water is exceedingly still, so much so, that it perfectly reflects back the surrounding vegetation with barely a ripple. Tom had dubbed this area the "Quiet Waters" as a young boy and I knew from his books that it had been a special teaching area to him. So too, it would turn out to be a very special place for me.

The exercises I did that Tuesday by the Quiet Waters all had to do with focusing on my interior feelings. How did I feel? Why was I feeling this way at this time? How did I feel about what I was feeling? It was a day on a psychologist's couch. I have never been very good at identifying feelings so it took intense focus and inner honesty for me to name them, to feel them, and to own them. In one exercise we were to heal an inner feeling that was negative. I was dwelling on my mother's passing and how I felt about that and so it came to pass that by the Quiet Waters I was able to heal my anger toward her, forgive her and be at peace with her memory.

At one point later that afternoon we were to journal how we felt. I wrote:

- Like a child
- Nervous but excited
- Overwhelmed
- Longing for answers
- Comfortable
- Needing to go forward with an open heart and mind
- Quiet
- Blessed

We were to then ask how our sit spot felt to us and what we sensed we might learn from this. Gazing upon the surface of the water I saw beauty in the reflection of the trees and scrub oak but then saw underneath it all that the current was strong and that was where the real change occurred. So too, within myself, I felt as though I was beginning to reflect the beauty of life around me in the "surface" of my relationships but also knew that the real changes were occurring deep within my very being. Psalm 46:10 came to my mind "Be still and know that I am God." God is God, I am the creature. A beloved creature to be sure, but being God was not my affair. As an addict I knew my tendency to want to be a god, my own god and other people's god. I sought attention and devotion and got depressed when either was not immediately given to me. It was no surprise then that as I sat there by the Quiet Waters that my relationship to God, whom I called my Abba (daddy) and the earth, whom I called Imma (mother) was clarified.

I wrote in my journal,

> "I always seem to be in a hurry, rushing to get somewhere. I have yet to learn the value of waiting or I am still learning it now. Waiting is not about patience, which is still to be goal-focused. Waiting is about listening, learning, growing and changing so that when it is time to move, I am ready."

> "God's power is given to those who seek it and are prepared and ready for it. To be ready is to be willing to serve."

> "A little water bug can cast concentric rings on the surface of the water that reach all the way to the farthest shore."

It was time for lunch and I was in an incredibly introspective mood. Fortunately so was everybody else. Later that day we would engage in exercises of discerning presence through the Temple of the soul. This was a deeper sense of awareness than I had previously experienced. It was almost tangible, but that is because the Temple of the soul has a strong connection to the physical world. After a few more exercises I wrote in my journal that,

"In Presence there is a sense of what is; in Temple there is a sense of what is to become. In Temple it is a question of my relation to the outside of self; in Presence I am aware of the 'outside' of self. It is hard to categorize this Temple stuff. I don't seem to have pegs (psychological or otherwise) to hang it on."

I was as open and vulnerable as I could be; and the skeptic was keeping a distant but watchful eye. Yet no matter how hard I tried I just could not find words to express what was happening. Back in Philosophy 7 we had learned how to listen to a plant communicate a medicinal value. Tom informed us that oak has five medicinal properties but that only two of them could be discerned by Presence; the other three could only be discerned in the soul. Can you guess what the next exercise was to be? Without questioning we were to sit down beside an oak and surrender. I was no longer astonished when I sensed things and although I did not get five answers I did receive a lot of information from that oak on its uses as an astringent, a blood thinner and a digestive. The rest of Tuesday was taken up with exercises on surrendering while we sat in the rain on Prophecy Hill and Spirit Hill.

Wednesday morning brought the promise of sunshine, although that promise never quite materialized, and the ground was damp from the previous evening's rain. Once again we spent the day engaging numerous exercises testing the limits of our skills as we listened deep inside, continued to journal, discussed and meditated on what we were learning. Thursday morning brought real sunshine bright and beautiful. The coffee seemed especially good. We worked on our Inner Vision for a good part of the morning hours.

At one point we were to go to our sit area to build a little fire and let it burn down a bit. At the point where we would add wood, we were instead to add a prayer and then add the wood. In our prayer we were to ask a question. I no longer remember my question but I recorded my "answer" as follows:

> "I need to create space, both internal space and 'space' when I am teaching. Space in a fire allows for oxygen to get in. My inner self is dense and needs to expand to go through a kind of 'big bang' and make room for the distinct parts. There is a universe within being born. In my teaching I need to focus on making intellectual space so that people can breathe, so the fires of inspiration can burn brightly."

I can vividly recall when I went to place the small twigs on the fire that I had packed it too tightly and it was struggling to stay lit. Using another twig I opened space for the fire to breathe and burn. That was when I felt a "BIG BANG" inside of me and I could perceive a whole universe. Just as there was a whole universe that existed outside of me, so too there existed one within. I felt expansive as though I could be everything everywhere all at once and yet still be me. Again words fail me.

Edgar is a member of the church I currently attend and he has remarked that while he really enjoys my teaching it is "like drinking from a fire hose." Last year when I was traveling and speaking in Australia, the exact same metaphor was used by someone else. So when the expansion happened and I was reminded of my teaching style it made good sense that I did not need to say everything all at once in a talk but could learn how to say what needed to be said and that future teaching times would take care of the rest. I thought that the 'big bang' was going to be my big experience of the week. I felt liberated and whole. I was content. I did not need anything else or any great epiphanies to make my week. Yet still there was more to come.

Back when I was a pastor in the early 1990's, a young woman came to our church. I would later be asked to meet her therapist. Dr Bilich had a frank conversation with me about Theresa. It turned out she had been diagnosed as a multiple personality. Nowadays it is referred to as Dissociative Identity Disorder but back then it was known as Multiple Personality Disorder. She had been horribly abused as a child and as a result Theresa had some twenty personalities, some more formed than others. I came to know about eight of them quite well and we became good friends. When she wanted to join our church I said to her that, by herself, she would constitute 20% of our total church membership! I just hoped they all tithed. Dr. Bilich and two of Theresa's friends have written a book documenting how clergy and therapists can work together with persons who are diagnosed with DID. It is titled *Shared Grace*.

Before that, in my Jungian days, I had learned how to identify various "parts" of myself and so was not surprised that people could have different parts. So too Tom observed that Grandfather's view of the human constituted numerous 'parts.' I have already mentioned the various aspects of our self using Grandfather's terminology: there is the physical self, the Life Force self, the Spirit Self. There is also our Presence self and our Subconscious self as well as our Temple self. Each part of our person is perceived as a whole, from within its own perspective. Wonderful I thought, but it made no sense to me and what good does it do? Did we all have multiple personalities?

As I sat there by my little fire next to the Quiet Waters suddenly I saw myself, over and over again, outside myself. What was totally weird was that each self was a different color. There was a green me, a red me, a gold me, a white me, a purple me and one that was invisible but I knew was there. All of them were me. The weirdest part came when they started talking to me. Oh boy, for sure, "the men in white coats were coming to take me away, ha-ha, ho-ho, hee-hee, to the funny farm where life is beautiful all the time…"

To this day I do not recall what it was we discussed but it seemed like a long getting-to- know-you kind of conversation. They knew all about me, that is, the me that I knew as me although I didn't know about them. Unlike a person who suffers from DID and whose personalities all have different names, each one of my colorful selves was Michael. Together they were Michael. Together we were all Michael. Even now as I write this I sense them peering over my shoulder.

Unlike my ego, or myself as I know myself, they are truth tellers. They do not deceive. They are my advocates, my advisors, my friends. For several weeks following Philosophy 9, I had many conversations with them and sensed their presence all the time. Gradually that faded. I called them "The Colored Men."[4] Purple Man advised me to treat Lorri like a queen. When I told her this she took an instant liking to Purple Man. I was disappointed that I had no Blue Man or else I would have gone to New York City to apply

---

[4] The term I use "Colored Men" is not to be construed in a racial fashion. It expresses the many-hued rainbow colored selves as I experienced them; it is an expression or metaphor of internal psychological diversity, and nothing more.

for the Blue Man group. (The Colored Men don't think that is very funny. C'mon boys, it's just a joke. No worries.)

Each part of myself had manifested itself as a whole of myself by a different color. Together we make up a rainbow. Like light which can be refracted into various colors so too I discovered that the same could be said of my self. In the past two years I have had little conscious awareness of the Colored Men, until a few weeks ago.

I was in a class just last month where we were discerning intent. Our exercise was simple. The entire class gathered in an area and each group from the class was to take turns and go off to decide whether they would come back to the group feeling rage, peace, threat or hatred. We would then discern that emotion and write it down. After a few minutes the group leader would announce what they had chosen and were feeling so we could know whether we were right or wrong and make corrections to our discernment process. I had been struggling with this kind of thing all day in exercise after exercise. In the group sit, I went three for three, three wrong answers. I despaired. I would never get this. Suddenly Red Man appeared and said "Did you ask us for help?" What was he doing here? "No," I replied, "I didn't even think of it." Red Man and the others shared with me a mental picture I could use where we locked arms around one another's waists in a straight line and dipped our faces together into the slipstream of emotion. After that I went six for six, all correct answers!

At some point on Thursday afternoon we were to take a walk dwelling in the "sacred silence" from Grandfather's camp to Hell then to Spirit Hill. When I say we I mean the entire class but now I also mean me as a 'we.' The Colored Men were as real as anyone else around me. Every exercise after that I did as a group with them. Each of them had an individual role to play in any given exercise and I reveled in my new friends. Somehow they only seem to appear now when I am in great need, as happened at the last class, but if I am very attentive I can sense their presence and am thankful for them.

Later that afternoon, Tom talked about prayer. Tom is a vociferous critic of Christianity. His father was a "religious fanatic." I think Tom had the kind of relationship to his father that I had with my mother. So I am always a little surprised when Tom ventures onto my turf, the stuff of theology. I seem to listen with a far more critical ear when he does this. I was really surprised when he talked about how he did not know how to talk to God and when he had mentioned this to Grandfather as a young man Grandfather had replied, "Talk to the Great Mystery, grandson, the way you talk to me." This is exactly how Jesus talked about prayer! It is why when he prayed he always used the word 'Abba' which is the first word a child learns to call his or her daddy. It is a term of intimacy and respect. Grandfather and Jesus were on the same page about prayer! My heart rejoiced. The Colored Men all laughed. "Of course they would be on the same page," they said. Both Jesus and Grandfather knew the loving Creator of all Life and all that is life-giving.

There is no doubt that Grandfather was a shaman. Jesus, too, was a shaman. Not too long ago that might have been a controversial way of describing Jesus. Recent scholarship, however, gives some substance to reconsidering the potential shamanic background and mission of Jesus. Back in 1973 Jewish biblical scholar Geza Vermes was able to understand Jesus in the light of other healers and 'holy men' of his time (known as Hasidim).[5] In 1968 Jewish biblical scholar David Flusser had already placed Jesus within the category of a sage or wisdom teacher; in 1994 Christian New Testament scholar Ben Witherington III extended and deepened this type of analysis.[6] In 2000, New Testament scholar Bruce Chilton examined Jesus in the light of Jewish mystical traditions (known as Merkebah mysticism).[7] James Charlesworth of Princeton Theological Seminary has examined similarities and differences between Jesus and the ascetic group of his time known as Essenes.[8] This was a group familiar with medicinal use of plants and prophecy, two major components of shamanism. John the Baptist, Jesus' choice as his mentor appears on the scene manifesting a number of characteristics of a shaman.[9] Finally, from my perspective, one of the most exciting books to be recently published looks at Jesus in the light of a critical analysis of shamanism; Pieter Craffert has written an admirable study titled *The Life of a Galilean Shaman*.[10] The study of the shaman as a social type is very recent. In view of all this research it has been

---

[5] *Jesus the Jew* (London: Collins, 1973).

[6] David Flusser, *The Sage from Galilee* (Grand Rapids, 2007), was first published in German in 1968 and translated into English and published in Israel in 1997 (Jerusalem: Magnes Press, 1997); Ben Witherington III, *Jesus the Sage: The Pilgrimage of Wisdom* (Minneapolis: Augsburg Fortress, 1994).

[7] *Rabbi Jesus* (New York: Doubleday, 2000).

[8] *Jesus and the Dead Sea Scrolls* (New York: Doubleday, 1992).

[9] Robert L Webb, *John the Baptizer and Prophet* (Eugene: Wipf & Stock, 1991).

[10] (Eugene: Cascade Books, 2008).

important for me to understand Grandfather in the light of Jesus and Jesus in the light of Grandfather. Shamanism is an aspect of the story of both figures that I know I will pursue for years to come.

Finally, on Friday night the entire class shared in a very moving meditation sequence that began in a sweat lodge and ended up in Grandfather's camp. I was completely taken by surprise. Tom had taken this class farther than even he anticipated and together we had all somehow learned crucial lessons about being healers of ourselves, of others and of the earth. To say that I was transformed that week feels like an understatement. When Lorri and I got home we spent weeks discussing just what had happened to us and what it all meant for our ministry in Preaching Peace and how we could integrate all we had learned from Grandfather with all we had learned from Jesus.

If the Standard class was the Worst Week of My Life, then I would have to say that Philosophy 9 was one of the Best Weeks of My Life. I will never be able to go back and experience Philosophy 9 again. I wish I could, just like I wish I could read *The Lord of the Rings* again for the first time as well. My memories are strong though and I have my notebooks. After that horrible night in the weekend Scout Intensive Tom had growled at me, "Well, did you learn anything?"

If Tom should ever read this I hope he knows how much I appreciate all I have learned from him. Walking with Grandfather has been a real honor. Walking with Jesus has been the same. Walking with both of them together is empowering. I plan to take more classes from time to time. I hope that someday Tom offers us a Philosophy 10 course.

Finally, I can only pray that whenever I teach about Jesus that I do so with the same passion with which Tom teaches about Grandfather. If that is the case I will have fulfilled my calling and lived a blessed and fruitful life.

Epilogue

My friend, theologian James Alison, once told me that it is a miracle that I have accomplished what I have with my life and become the person I am today given all the handicaps under which I have labored. I have thought often about that and think *miracle* is the right word. God does beautiful things and he has put the right people in my life at the right time so that I may learn the lessons for each day. Today is the only day I have. For me there are only two important questions to ask daily: What will I learn today and what shall I practice today?

Practice makes perfect. I think Plato said that or maybe Socrates. Whether I am following Jesus or practicing what I have learned at The Tracker School, it is true that it takes practice. I am not very good at some of the skills I have learned only because I don't practice them enough. The same thing is true of life. The more I practice love, forgiveness, mercy, patience, peacemaking or any other virtue taught by Jesus, the better I get at it.

I wake each day with a new sense of wonder and gratitude. Life holds many mysteries which I am eager to explore. It may well be that I could have found my way to this openness to life through an exploration of some aspect of Christian theology I had neglected or taken a journey through Christian mysticism. Perhaps I could have learned it through Buddhism or another religious tradition, perhaps the Jewish Cabala or even yoga. I just happened to be dragged kicking and screaming into Grandfather's vision.

I am *not* an evangelist for the Tracker School. I have sought to be open and honest about my experiences of both Tom Brown Jr. and the Tracker School. My goal has been to tell my story and perhaps if you find yourself interested you will read Grandfather's story or maybe even be a little adventurous, purchase yourself a decent tent and take some classes at the Tracker School (**www.trackerschool.com**). At any rate, I pray that you will find yourself leaving the Empire of Little Intellectual Boxes that constrain and confine. Jesus called us to be as little children, imaginative, open and expectant that God is working in our world and waits for us to simply open our hearts and minds to the great Love that infuses all things.

I have written a book of Christian theology where I tell how I have learned to walk *The Jesus Driven Life*. This book is a complement to that one. Jesus is my Lord, my Savior, my brother. Grandfather is a mentor. He is not my savior or Lord. Yet, Wisdom comes in many forms; the Christian tradition is not the only place one can find Wisdom. With Wisdom comes peace, with peace, joy, with joy, wholeness. May wholeness be your life.

Shuna and Amen.

"EcoSpirituality"

Or What Happens When You Sit Down With A French Historian,
A Swiss Theologian And An Apache Shaman.

An Odyssey in Essay Form

November 2003
Michael Hardin
www.preachingpeace.org

A Presentation given to the Colloquium on Violence and Religion

"At a Lyceum, not long ago, I felt that the lecturer had chosen a
theme too foreign to himself, and so failed to interest me as much as
he might have done. He described things not in or near to his heart,
but toward his extremities and superficies. There was in this sense no
truly central or centralizing thought in the lecture. I would have had
him deal with privatest experience, as the poet does."
-Henry David Thoreau[11]

The proposition that mimetic theory had something to do with the
environment at first blush seemed, well, far fetched. Had we so
quickly run through the humanities that we now had to turn our
attention to something else? Or, perhaps, has the romp of mimetic
theory through the humanities not indeed set us up precisely for this
conference? For in the end, we are talking about ourselves, the
survival of the human race and the equally important survival of our
planet. And we all pray that we are not witnesses to the apocalyptic
scenario found in the gospels of the 'war of all against all', the
ultimate mimetic crisis.

That mimetic theory has to do with the environment, and thus with
us, indicates two areas of exploration, the cause and effects of

---

[11] *Walden and Other Writings*

negative mimesis and the cause and effects of positive mimesis.[12] The first are the negative effects of mimesis with regard to our use and abuse of the environment. Deforestation, water wars[13], stolen harvests[14], the toxification of the environment[15], the ozone hole and global warming[16], all of the waste at the bottom of our life source, the oceans and, oh, so much more. These are extraordinarily negative effects, all right, and they are all mimetically conceived.

Christians, as well as others, might conceivably turn their attention at

---

[12] From the beginning of my use of mimetic theory I have sought to ask about both positive and negative mimesis. Dr. Ed Hallsten of North Park Theological Seminary and I spent countless hours one year discussing all of the possibilities we could think of. His expertise in neuro-psychology and psychiatry allowed me to think outside the training a typical Seminary candidate might have. I will always remember those conversations, with a grateful heart, as my seminal baptism into mimetic theory.

[13] Vandana Singh. *Water Wars*

[14] Vandana Singh *Stolen Harvest* (Cambridge: South End Press, 2000).

[15] We can date our awareness of the toxification of the environment to the publication of Rachel Carson's *Silent Spring* (Cambridge: Riverside Press) in 1962. Frank Graham *Since Silent Spring* (New York: Fawcett, 1970) chronicles the substantive debate that arose around her revelations in the 1960's. Some 40 years later, it seems as though far too many 'civilized' people ignore the consequences of our continual poisoning of the Earth. The environment is just another political hot potato like war, foreign policy, trade, the economy and the like. Those who take an interest in the earth are pejoratively referred to as tree huggers, whale lovers, left wing liberals or new age fanatics. More's the pity.

[16] It has recently been said that it is possible that we can actually reverse the growing ozone hole. The United States evidently does not care. Witness U.S. refusal to sign the Kyoto treaty as well as the Bush administration's utter disdain for the environment. In a recent radio interview Robert F. Kennedy Jr., argued that the Bush administration has reversed almost 40 years of ecological policy since Carson's revelations. Every single federal law that was designed to protect the environment has been subverted or changed.

---

this point to Walter Wink's *The Powers*[17]. In these three volumes, Walter lays out a very convincing case that we must broaden our perspective on the many-layeredness of the mimetic 'principalities and powers.' The State, corporation politics, economics, media, violence and religion are all expressions of darker powers[18]. From the perspective of Christian dogmatics, Walter joined together what theology had rent asunder, in its separation of ethics from eschatology. But this also meant that one could talk about positive mimesis. This, of course, for the Christian, means taking the life of Jesus seriously.

But how do we do that in an age of skepticism and nihilism? I guess I'm a bit of a pragmatist. If it doesn't work, I'm not interested. So I test things, I work problems through to solutions. I say to myself, this works, this makes sense. I'm reasonably certain that I am sane, ergo, I trust my perceptions. I feel no pressure to be either a skeptic or a nihilist. I've been down the Cartesian road many times, and eventually it got to be a long boring ride every time. I have often wondered how René's theory felt for others when they first saw its implications for their discipline. For me, it was a rush. When I survey the array of literature written in the past twenty years on mimetic theory, I am astounded[19]. I see mimetic theory being applied

---

[17] Walter Wink. *Naming The Powers, Unmasking The Powers, Engaging The Powers* (Philadelphia: Fortress Press). See also Vernard Eller *Christian Anarchy: Jesus Primacy Over The Powers* (Grand Rapids: Eerdmans, 1987).

[18] Mimetic theorists have major disagreements among themselves as to where to draw the line beyond which society and culture move from good violence to bad violence. For me there is no line because there is no good violence.

[19] A comprehensive (although not exhaustive) bibliography can be found on the website for the Colloquium on Violence and Religion.

all over the place, in short, across the domain of the principalities and powers.

Is there a mimetic theorist among us who did not think about the scapegoat after 9/11? Is there a theorist here among us who, when reading the news, has to worry about running out of examples of negative mimesis?

Up to this point in our academic conversation mimetic theory has made enormous and important contributions to anthropological studies. But at this conference, the rubber meets the road, for what it is we confront in a mimetically-conceived humanity is a species that is self-destructive. The proof lies in the fact that we have been put on notice: the planet is in very bad shape, in fact it is dying because WE ARE KILLING HER. We persist in destroying the very environment that feeds and nurtures us. Native Americans said that the white man starves his grandchildren to feed his children. How stupid are we as a species anyway? Can I get an Amen?

We might ask about the influences that shaped such a way of viewing the creation. What is the natural world and what is it there for? We have been programmed to believe that humans are to dominate the planet. We are the superior species. We act as though the Earth and ourselves are completely separate entities, as though we are not of the same substance. The species that was meant to be the caretakers of the earth has turned into her killer.

So, yes, mimetic theory has something to say with regard to the environment. The exposure of the principalities and powers is why we are gathered. And mimetic theory does that. In pointing out these lies, it exposes the liar. But we are not without hope. For we also know there can be positive mimesis. Raymund Schwager opened the door for us to connect Jesus' life with positive mimesis[20]. Willard Swartley has followed this up utilizing the valuable language of 'discipleship[21].' James Allison has demonstrated positive mimesis in Jesus' spirituality[22].

I knew that I could connect all of this to something near to my heart: the Trinitarian conversations I have had over the years, mostly with Karl Barth. Yes, Barth has been dead since 1968. But I find myself returning over and over again to the *Church Dogmatics* as a conversation partner[23]. Here, too, I found positive mimesis done in the context of dogmatic Christology. Jesus' humanity was taken seriously. Indeed, it was *The Humanity of God*[24] that truly captivated Karl Barth.

Then, a final piece of the puzzle came to me a few years ago in serendipitous fashion. My daughter and my wife encouraged me to

---

[20] Raymund Schwager, *Must There Be Scapegoats?* (New York: Harper & Row, 1987), *Jesus In The Drama Of Salvation* (New York: Crossroad, 1999), *Jesus of Nazareth* (New York: Crossroad, 1998).

[21] Willard Swartley, *Violence Renounced* (Telford: Pandora, 2000).

[22] James Alison *Raising Abel* (New York: Crossroad, 1996). Although I occasionally don't find myself on the same page as Alison, nevertheless *Raising Abel* will remain important because it brought to the forefront of our consciousness that we have to stop talking about what Jesus believed about God, as though God was as abstract for Jesus as God is for us. Not so. Jesus had a spirituality that can be explored in the Gospels but it takes more than just scientific criticism to discern this. It also requires the commitment and discipline to go on a spiritual journey oneself and discover what Jesus discovered. This is his gift to us.

[23] Karl Barth *Church Dogmatics* (London, T&T Clark).

[24] Karl Barth *The Humanity of God* (London: Collins, 1961).

166

read a book. If I had a nickel for every book someone told me to read I would be rich. Now one does not lightly refuse the women of the house. So I read the story of Grandfather[25], born into the Apache Nation, of the Lipan tribe, shortly after the American civil war and who lived until around 1970. Just then the 'light bulb' of positive mimesis went on again and I began to see that just as it is possible to speak of positive mimesis in the language of inter-personal relationships, it was also possible to see the gains that a positive mimesis would bring to spirituality and Christian existence and especially to our relationship with the creation.

René Girard, Karl Barth and Grandfather are the three figures I would like to juxtapose. They are a trio of mentors, if you will. I believe I can correctly assume that you are all acquainted with the life and work of René Girard. So I can presuppose this. Karl Barth will need some introduction, though many of you will be acquainted with his reputation and theology. But I would be surprised if any of you knew of Grandfather or "Stalking Wolf", as his tribe called him. Therefore I will be supplying biographical information about him to

---

[25] Tom Brown Jr. writes about Grandfather in every single one of his eighteen books. He has narrated Grandfather's story in *Grandfather* (New York: Berkley, 1994). Tom kept extensive journals throughout his time with Grandfather and is there is plenty of oral tradition still circulating. Old Jersey "Pineys" that knew Grandfather have been interviewed by Kevin Reeve. New stories about Grandfather are one of the more fascinating aspects of being able to share in the class experience at The Tracker School. Grandfather's birth name was Nuachano; he was later 'given' the name Stalking Wolf. 'Grandfather' is what Tom called Stalking Wolf. It should be noted that in native tradition the title Grandfather does not necessarily indicate blood lineage, but is expressive of respect for wisdom.

the extent that is available[26].

Kierkegaard said that life is lived forward but it is only understood backward. In this essay, I will weave many strands together, each of which illumines the other. Looking back on almost fifty years of life with the Church and theology, I can see a tapestry where previously I had only seen chaos. Unlike most academic essays, I believe that when talking about the creation, the more personal we get, the more authentic our speech becomes. In short, this essay is an exercise in self-understanding. It is an odyssey. As such I propose to navigate what I see as profound consequences for Christian theology when René Girard, Karl Barth and Grandfather are brought together. Very different folk they are from very different backgrounds, yet here we will see persons whose theories form a unity of perspective.[27]

---

[26] My sole source of 'historical information' regarding Grandfather is Tom Brown Jr. Tom's friend Rick (Stalking Wolf's blood grandson) died in a horse accident in Europe many years ago. The historian in me wants to cringe at some sense of paucity but frankly, the cumulative evidence is overwhelming and in my best judgment, Tom is accurately passing on Grandfather's story, legacy and vision. The Lipan Apache are among the least known and written about in literature on the Apache. Much more familiar are the Chiricachuas, the Jicarillas, the Kiowa-Apache and the Mescaleros. I scoured the databases at the Research Center of the Mashantucket Pequot Nation and could find almost nothing about the Lipan. Part of the reason for this is the separation of the tribe during the smallpox outbreaks of the 19th century. Grandfather's people, led by Coyote Thunder were completely separated and isolated not only from the encroaching civilization of the white man but also from other Apaches. The need to find suitable habitation with water, fuel and food sources that would remain isolated was the task of the Scout. See Tom Brown Jr., *The Way of the Scout* (New York: Berkley, 1997).

[27] I remind the reader that this is not a scholarly essay in the usual sense. Early reviewers of this essay did not find the argument tightly woven. But then, neither am I. It is an 'odyssey in essay form.' If you seek a detailed argument this paper is not for you. If however, the convergence of anthropological theory, Christian theology and Native American shamanism interests you, this paper is a modest proposal for articulating a way to conceive our relation to the creation and the Creator.

Each of us has a story to tell about the way we have learned from mimetic theory. Most of us have integrated mimetic theory into our professional disciplines and have found it profitable as an illuminating tool. And each of us, in our own way, has been exposed to the effects of mimesis in our own lives, so we also value mimetic theory for its wisdom. For those who have ears to hear, it is the wisdom of the ages. Nothing is secret, nothing is hidden. This is not something discovered as much as uncovered, ergo, revealed.

As I have previously mentioned, one of the more astonishing aspects of mimetic theory is its application to every form of human discourse, every discipline, every walk of life. Mimetic theory is a gold mine. Those of us gathered here are simply the first ones at Sutter's Mill, but the word has already gotten out and many others are on their way. We have barely tapped the rich vein of gold that is mimetic theory. We are so grateful to René for having the courage to ask the tough questions even in the face of the virtually complete disapproval of his academic peers. It takes courage to ask the important questions for these questions are usually the stuff of life.

But the floodgates have been opened and we have the Colloquium on Violence and Religion to thank for that. These yearly gatherings and the research and dedication of so many like minded souls has proven that not only is mimetic theory here to stay, but it has a stake in what can only be termed the truth. Those of us who have appreciated the insights of mimetic theory do not use it as simply another theory in an avant-garde sort of way.

In the discipline of theology, mimetic theory has laid a strong challenge to previously held Christian orientations. On my website:

www.preachingpeace.org, I have utilized the many and wonderful publications of the 'Girardians[28].' Christian theology, for the most part, has been exposed as the emperor with no clothes. But there are reasons for this, not the least of which is the covert influence of negative mimesis and its effects on early Christian theology and church practice[29]. We can no longer afford to simply parrot the ecclesial party line. It is important to apply mimetic theory across the board to the science of religion in all of its multitudinous sub-disciplines.

What we find when we apply mimetic theory to Christian theology is that there is a deep and lasting influence of dualism that runs through virtually all Western Christian theology. Christian dualists or Gnostics, as is well known, denigrate the material world and exalt the spiritual or inner man. They are anti-creation. They perceive the creation to be flawed. Who is to blame? A lesser god, a demiurge, and there you have it, the creator and the creation are rejected as unworthy of respect. Philip Lee has clearly and coherently articulated the thesis that modern American Protestantism and

---

[28] **www.preachingpeace.org**. This site was conceived at the COV&R conference held at Purdue in June of 2002. Jeff and I had been having intense discussions for two years on many interrelated theological topics. Our concerns merged after September 11, 2001 when we realized just how far the Church had moved away from the gospel of Jesus. PreachingPeace.org is essentially tackling several interrelated topics: 1) those having to do with the historical Jesus, 2) those having to do with the development of Christology, 3) the nature of the gospels and the gospel tradition, 4) the role of mimetic theory in biblical interpretation and its hermeneutical application, 5) the consequences of the aforementioned research for systematic theology, particularly in the Christian understanding of God as trinity, 6) the importance of the Anabaptist emphasis on discipleship and 7) Christian spirituality.

[29] See my essay "The Biblical Testaments as a Marriage of Convenience" at www.preachingpeace.org.

ancient Gnosticism are virtually identical[30]. It is the contemporary Babylonian captivity of the Church. It is also true, in one degree or another, for the greater part of Christian theology and history, both orthodox and heretical[31].

The effects of dualism can be found virtually everywhere in Christian theology not the least in that we attribute to the Creator a malice that is not really there at all. This malice is all over the western doctrine of election and can be found especially in certain atonement theories as Anthony Bartlett has shown[32]. The malice of God becomes translated into 'acts of God' (a disputable actuarial category) and the creation is seen as dark, foreboding, untamed, something to be conquered. Yes, the church has contributed to western culture's devaluation of creation. And look what we have done to Her (Gaia). Environmentalists are not doomsday forecasters. They are prophets. The human species is dealing a mortal wound to

---

[30] *Against the Protestant Gnostics* (London: Oxford, 1988).

[31] The finest book I have read on the history of dualism is Yuri Stoyanov The Other God (New Haven: Yale, 2000). It stands apart in that the comprehensive research that went into this book is so excellently distilled. Stoyanov leaves no stone unturned.

[32] *Cross Purposes* (Harrisburg: Trinity Press, 2001). We might note here that there are discussions of the relationship between mimetic theory and the atonement at **www.preachingpeace.org**. We tend to follow those who value the *Christus Victor* model in some combination with the *Exemplary* model, most notably found in the Mennonite tradition. A fine Reformed perspective on the atonement is given by Jacques De Senarclens, *Heirs of the Reformation* (Philadelphia: Westminster, 1959). De Senarclens however, finds the heart of the debate in the question "Who accomplishes our salvation, he or we? There seems to be no third possibility. Jesus is either our Saviour or our Example." This either/or need not be imported into atonement theory if the atonement is coordinated with the incarnation as suggested by Robin Collins "Girard and Atonement: An Incarnational Theory of Mimetic Participation" in Willard Swartley ed., *Violence Renounced* (Telford: Pandora Press, 2000).

the earth. Humans have become a plague on the earth. We can see that Christian theology has been a major contributor to our pillaging of the planet. It need not be so.

One of the important assets Karl Barth brings to the table is that he is one of the most significant theologians of the twentieth century. He has been compared to Luther, Augustine and Irenaeus. He has been called a modern church father[33]. Barth had to deal with this malice that had been attributed to the Creator. The traditional structure of theology demanded it as virtually every Western theological system has Augustine's fingerprints all over it. Barth is able to get behind, and thus beyond, Augustine by viewing election through a christological lens where God in God's freedom does not reject humanity but self-elects to be rejected by humanity. This rejection has a specific history with a specific people and so Barth begins his exegesis of the biblical doubles that function typologically of the

---

[33] Among the literature I value see Hugh Ross Mackintosh *Types of Modern Theology* (New York: Scribers, 1937); Hans Urs von Balthasar *The Theology of Karl Barth* (New York: Holt, Reinhart and Winston, 1971); Thomas Torrance *Karl Barth: An Introduction to His Early Theology 1916-1931* (London: SCM Press, 1962); Eberhard Busch Karl Barth: His Life from Letters and Autobiographical Texts (Philadelphia: Fortress, 1976); other helpful resources include Eberhard Jungel *Karl Barth: A Theological Legacy* (Philadelphia: Westminster, 1986) and *The Doctrine of the Trinity* (Grand Rapids: Eerdmans, 1976); Jeffrey C. Pugh *The Anselmic Shift* (New York: Peter Lang, 1990); Martin Rumscheidt *Revelation & Theology: An Analysis of the Barth Harnack Correspondence of 1923* (London: Cambridge University Press, 1972); Charles T Waldrop *Karl Barth's Christology* (Berlin: Walter de Gruyter, 1984); Thomas Torrance *Karl Barth: Biblical & Evangelical Theologian* (Edinburgh: T&T Clark, 1990); Mark L. Wallace *The Second Naivete: Barth, Ricoeur and the New Yale Theology* (Macon: Mercer University Press, 1990); George Hunsinger *How To Read Karl Barth* (New York: Oxford, 1991) and *Karl Barth and Radical Politics* (Philadelphia: Westminster, 1976).

electing God that elects sinners but rejects sin.[34] This God freely chooses to be for humanity, there is no God against us. This was an important theological breakthrough; it asserted that there is no God behind God, there is only one God. This is also known as Rahner's rule: the economic trinity is the immanent trinity and vice versa. Much modern Christianity on the other hand is Sabellian in disguise[35].

In order, however, to really appreciate the legacy of Barth, it is essential to notice the complete freedom with which Barth wrote about God's freedom. In the face of a lot of 'God against us' kinds of thinking and preaching, Barth reached back and articulated the thesis that God is for us. God in complete freedom chooses to be for us, and for Barth, this is seen in the love shared with us in the person of Jesus Christ.

In the *Church Dogmatics* (12 volumes, over 8,000 pages), Barth revisits virtually every major theological question asked by the Church in its long history. And from its initial publication in 1932 to

---

[34] *Church Dogmatics II/2.* The thesis statement of paragraph 32 reads, "The doctrine of election is the sum of the Gospel because of all the words that can be said and heard it is the best: that God elects man; that God is for man too the One who loves in freedom. It is grounded in the knowledge of Jesus Christ because He is both the electing God and elected man in One. It is part of the doctrine of God because originally God's election of man is a predestination not merely of man but of Himself. Its function is to bear basic testimony to eternal, free and unchanging grace as the beginning of all the ways and works of God."

[35] Sabellius was a second century 'heretic' who taught that "God the Son is nowhere mentioned in the Old Testament; the divine Sonship was revealed only at the incarnation; why suppose that the Person of Jesus Christ embodies any new disclosure about the being of God?" God is "one reality with variable appearance." G. L. Prestige, *Fathers and Heretics* (London: SPCK, 1940). Thus, there is a God behind God.

---

the fragment on baptism in 1967[36], there is a remarkable consistency in its thought. At the heart of that consistency is the consistency of God, God's faithfulness. This was the good news of the gospel that Barth heard. God is on the side of humanity. More than that, God is our champion.

What has been important for me, as I have read Barth, is to watch him as he wrestles with Augustine. I wouldn't want to get in the ring with Augustine. So I appreciate that Barth has done this. For example, Barth's doctrine of election still retains both election and rejection; but it is not humanity in general that is elected or rejected. Specifically, God chooses to elect himself to be rejected in the humanity of Jesus, so that he may elect us to be with Jesus in his resurrection. The God of the gospel is all about self-giving love.

In his volume on creation, Barth comes at God the Creator from a fresh perspective. Barth sees in the two creation narratives (Genesis 1-2:4 and 2:5ff) two sides of a coin. The shift from El in the first creation narrative to YHWH in the second narrative signals to Barth that one reality is being discussed two ways. The reason for this is because they belong together. So Barth brings into conversation God the Creator and God the Redeemer. Inasmuch as we are speaking of one God, Barth can say that the creation is the external basis of the covenant and the covenant is the internal basis of creation.

By insisting that creation and covenant belong together and cannot be separated, Barth deals a mortal blow to any form of Marcionism.

---

[36] The 1960's saw René developing mimetic theory and publishing *Violence and the Sacred*, Barth completing his life's work and Grandfather mentoring Tom. The 60's were a very special time.

174

Marcion separated the Creator from the Redeemer. By contrast, in these opening narratives, Barth recognizes that the God who creates is the God who has redeemed a very specific people. This drama of redemption recorded in the Hebrew Scriptures is full of God's promise to be faithful to His people. And the fulfillment of all God's promises occurred in Jesus Christ. Barth's reconciliatory hermeneutic is at work even here. Unlike the way in which Calvin, e.g., linked the Testaments, Barth brings the two Testaments together by weaving them into the Trinitarian history of God. Creation and redemption cannot be separated.

The consequence of this Barth calls "The Yes of God to creation.' I know of no other Christian systematic theology that accents the doctrine of creation this way.[37] This Yes! of God for Barth is the essential consequence of the Covenant-Creator's act of creating. God saw that everything was good. Barth asserts that the creation is a benefit for us. The Creator is a beneficial God in an intentional relationship with us.[38] By bringing covenant and creation into a relationship, Barth has provided a method for us to understand what Grandfather calls the relation between the flesh and the spirit or as I might put, it "the wilderness of creation and the wilderness of the

---

[37] Daniel Migliore of Princeton Theological Seminary is an exception. While not a systematic theology as such *Faith Seeking Understanding* clearly articulates the necessity of taking ecological considerations seriously when framing a doctrine of creation. But then, Migliore was influenced by Barth.

[38] *Church Dogmatics* III/1, 331-32. "We cannot understand the divine creation otherwise than as benefit. We are not free to think and speak in this matter otherwise or even uncertainly or equivocally. The Christian apprehension of creation requires and involves the principle that creation is benefit. It shows us God's good pleasure as the root, the foundation and the end of divine creation. It suggests the peace with which God separated and protected what He truly willed from what He did not will, and therefore from the unreal. It implies that God Himself, in and with the beginning of all things, decided for his creation and made Himself the responsible Guarantor of it. Creation, as it is known by the Christian, is benefit."

soul." There can be a direct correlation between experience of the Creator in the wilderness, Jesus in worship and the Spirit-that-moves-in-all-things. The Creator has covenanted for us to be with us. The gospel asserts that the Creator did not abandon humanity but so imbued one life that it could be said that the behavior of the Rabbi from Nazareth was the behavior of God. Jesus is not unique because he is divine. Jesus is not the only one to ever teach about the Creator. He is distinct in the non-retributive posture and spirituality of his mission. And therefore, he brings to revelation a truly different God, a God not created by mimetic victimage, the Covenant Creator, the 'Abba.'

The Church has made the mistake of trying to argue for Jesus' identity with God in terms of Hellenistic philosophy, in terms of an already posited dualism. Identity in Judaism however focuses on behavior. It is Jesus' behavior that is at stake in the question of his relationship with God not just some metaphysical equation. The New Testament does not ask "Is Jesus like God?" This is the question asked by those 'outside', who presuppose they know God but not Jesus. The New Testament asks the question: "Is God like Jesus?" What is startling and new about the gospel is that it brings to the forefront of our awareness that it is possible to say that in the behavior of Jesus of Nazareth we see the very character of the covenant Creator.

So where do we go from here? If mimetic theory helps us to understand the cause of our relentless consumerist lifestyle and its deleterious effects on the planet and Christian theology takes a lesson from Barth and courageously advances the thesis that our Abba, the Creator is merciful, then we might ask how we can now be reconciled with our own flesh, the earth.

From the outset, we must confess that we are hermeneutically narrative through the eyes of a persecutor and that we have been sucked into an anti-Christian way of thinking precisely by the Church. These early Genesis narratives are instructional not only for what they contribute to the deconstruction of mythology, they also carry an important dimension of positive mimesis. Dietrich Bonhoeffer has shown us that the 'image of God' in Genesis means that we are created in relationship.[39] Our relationships are as real as we are. Or, we *are* our relationships. Or perhaps one could say that we are interdividual?

In our relationship to the creation, Douglas John Hall has reminded us in his many books that any 'dominion' humans were to have over the earth was as that of stewards. We were meant to be careful caretakers of God's good creation, not its lords[40]. This creation-stewardship is part and parcel of the larger servant/slave motif found in the Jesus tradition as well as the Apostle Paul. Service is the essential category by which we were meant to be in relation to the creation, each other, and the Creator.

---

[39] *Creation and Fall* (London, SCM Press, 1959).

[40] See especially *Imaging God* (Grand Rapids: Eerdmans, 1986). In his 1978 address upon accepting the Templeton Foundation Prize for Progress in Religion, Thomas Torrance theologically describes humanity's relationship to the creation as priesthood in *The Ground and Grammar of Theology* (Belfast: Christian Journals Ltd., 1980). The utilization of this category is important not only on an intellectual level, which is important for Torrance, but also in our approach to the creation itself. We will sacrifice the creation all day long as she gives her life for us to feed us. Priesthood is the theological way of expressing the Native American understanding of caretaking our Mother Earth. It is something we all share (hence it is a priesthood of all believers) and it is characterized by gratitude (Eucharist).

In our intellectual arrogance we all too frequently understand nature as chemical reactions, electrical impulses and mathematical equations. We are capable of slicing and dicing the tiniest aspects of the physical world, from the pion to the gene and we are also capable of projecting mathematical hypotheses billions of years into the future. Everything science has to say about the natural world may well be true but it is not truth. Truth is more than just scientific explanation.

On the other hand, the natural world is an aesthetic proof of God for molecular biologist and theologian Alistair McGrath[41]. For McGrath there is an order, a harmony, a sense of transcendence nature brings. The beauty of nature is signaling us all of the time that we are in the presence of Something greater. Everyone has some experience of this. This experience is as true as that of scientific explanation but together they do not constitute the truth. Science and theology do not yet know the creation as a gift.

All Christian theology; whether white or black, male or female, Catholic or Protestant, medieval or modern, North American, Asian, African, liberal or conservative or anything else is civilized theology.[42] Even the New Testament is urban.[43]

---

[41] *The Enchantment of Nature* (New York: Doubleday, 2002)

[42] I am not aware of a single Christian theologian who practices the ancient ways. I confess to having limited knowledge of Native American-Christian dialogue. Two interesting books from quite different perspectives and times that I found helpful are Julia M. Seton *The Gospel of the Redman* (Santa Fe: Seton Village, 1937) and William Stolzman *The Pipe and Christ: A Christian-Sioux Dialogue* (Chamberlain: Tipi Press, 1986).

[43] Wayne Meeks *The First Urban Christians.*

The human experience of virtually all Western theologians is sharply defined by the simple fact that they were born into, lived, and died in the context of civilization. To be sure, there are bright beacons in the Christian tradition that reflect the virtues and glory of time with the creation. Anthony and elements of Egyptian monasticism, Celtic spirituality and St Francis are a few notable examples. So what is it that appears to be missing in so much of Christianity? Part of the answer lies in what we lost as humans as we became 'civilized' or as mimetic theorists might put it when we succumbed to the generative mimetic scapegoating mechanism.

The Genesis narrative indicates that an aspect of the 'cursed existence' was the transition for humans from wilderness (the garden) to civilization (Cain's city). Jacques Ellul offers a penetrating reading of this text.[44] He points out the connections to be made in the developing relation between the dominance of technology and urban civilization. Technology, or *the appropriation of technique as an exercise of power,* begins to separate us from the

---

[44] *The Meaning of the City* (Grand Rapids: Eerdmans, 1970). In addition see *The Technological Society* (New York: Vintage, 1964); *The Technological System* (New York: Continuum, 1980); *The Technological Bluff* (Grand Rapids: Eerdmans, 1990); *The Betrayal of the West* (New York: Seabury, 1978); *The Political Illusion* (New York: Random House, 1967); *The New Demons* (New York: Seabury, 1975). Mimetic theorists might also take note of the congruencies between Ellul and Girard in Ellul's *Violence* (New York: Seabury, 1969). Girard's analysis of mimesis fits hand in glove with Ellul's analysis of the consequences of technique. It would appear from Ellul's books that he read Girard's *Things Hidden* sometime in the 1980's. He appreciatively utilizes Girard's insights on the covetous dynamics of mimesis. See *Jesus and Marx* (Grand Rapids: Eerdmans, 1988) and *Anarchy and Christianity* (Grand Rapids: Eerdmans, 1988).

earth.[45] Ellul's warnings about the dangers of technique have gone largely unheeded and worse still is that Christianity is falling in lock step with civilization and thus, with the powers of the victimage mechanism. And so the Church continues to contribute to our corporate human journey away from the creation. What does this mean for us? Shoshone Glenn Wasson puts it this way:

> "In Indian terms there is no equation in dollars for the loss of a way of life...you cannot equate dollars to lives. The redmen are the last people on Earth who speak on behalf of all living things. The bear, the deer, the sagebrush have no one else to speak for them. The animals and the plants were put here by the Great Spirit before he put the humans here. There is a story the old people tell about the white men, that they are like children. They want this and that, they want everything they see, like it's their first time on Earth. The white men have all of these tools but they don't know how to use them properly. The white people try to equate national defense with human lives. There can never be an equation between the dollar bill and living things – the fish, the birds, the deer, the clean air, clean water. There is no way of comparing them...The white people have no love for this land. If we human beings persist in what we are doing we

---

[45] See Jurgen Moltmann, *Experiences of God* (Philadelphia: Fortress, 1980). Moltmann has a quote that can be heard through the lens of Girard as well as that of Ellul. "When we try to get to know something by the methods of modern science, we know in order to achieve mastery, to dominate. *Scientia est potestas*, said Francis Bacon, 'knowledge is power,' For by means of science we take possession of the object, becoming what Descartes promised the scientist would become - *maitre et possesseur de la nature*, the master and possessor of nature. And then nature becomes mute."

will become like a bad cancer on Mother Earth. If we don't stop ourselves, something will stop us."[46]

Was there a time in our evolutionary history when in fact we were as close to the earth as were any of the animals and yet still somehow untouched by the effects of negative mimesis? Was there a time of peace where we had not yet learned pillaging and plundering?[47] Were we not developing the skills that would keep us alive? But with the dawn of so-called civilization these skills began to be passed on less and less. And now at the dawn of this new century, these skills have virtually vanished from memory.

Bob Johannes asks, or rather implores us, to reconsider our understanding of aboriginal skills and their value to our modern world.

"Much of what we know about the nature and management of natural resources in developed countries can be found in libraries. [Among native communities], however, much of it resides only in the heads of older men and women in the villages. Scientists have come to realize within the past few years that such knowledge concerning the forest, the garden, the plains, and the sea, is both encyclopedic and of major scientific value, particularly as it relates to natural resource management. But it is being lost rapidly as a result of westernization, industrialization, urbanization and the

---

[46] Cited in Jerry Mander, *In the Absence of the Sacred* (San Francisco: Sierra Books, 1991).

[47] Following the lines laid down by Riane Eisler in *The Chalice and The Blade*.

---

concomitant alienation of the young from their tradition...Recording this knowledge is an urgent matter. Allowing it to vanish amounts to throwing away centuries of priceless practical experience."[48]

Many of you have heard or read the story of Ishi, the Yahi Native American who only knew and practiced the ancient ways, the aboriginal skills[49]. The anthropologists who had custody of Ishi were beside themselves, for here, for the first time, was someone who practiced the skills that produced their ancient artifacts. Sadly, Ishi died just a few years later in 1916. He was the last 'wild man.' A small window had been opened. But with Ishi's passing the ancient ways were now lost to history. The white man had forbidden the practice of the ancient Native American ways and had taught the Native American to ostracize those who practiced these skills. On the dreary reservations the only hope was now the white man's hope. We had stripped the Native Americans of their land and thus their future. We made damn sure we civilized them so they could be just like us[50].

At about the time Ishi was discovered near the Lassen Mountains in California, Grandfather had already been wandering the Americas,

---

[48] Cited in Mander, *In the Absence of the Sacred.*

[49] Theodora Kroeber. *Ishi in Two Worlds* (University of California Press: Berkeley, 1964); Robert Heizer and Theodora Kroeber, ed., *Ishi the Last Yahi: A Documentary History* (University of California Press: Berkeley, 1979).

[50] James Wilson, *The Earth Shall Weep: A History of Native America* (New York: Atlantic Monthly Press, 1998); Howard Zinn, *A People's History of the United States* (New York: Harper Collins, 1999). See also Mander, *In the Absence of the Sacred* for some disturbing contemporary examples. Sadly, similar distress has been visited on aboriginal cultures around the planet.

from Argentina to Alaska and back and forth across North America. He had been trained in an elite Medicine Society, the way of the ancient Scouts. Grandfather was an anthropologist in his own way. He perceived his mission in much the same way a Levi-Strauss might have. He collected and distilled everything he could learn about the creation. Grandfather sought to find that which all human 'philosophies' had in common. And so, he sought out the old ones wherever he went to learn as many of the ancient skills from different native peoples as he could. He was a treasure trove of earth skills. He learned from the best of the best. He knew Geronimo. He spent his entire life learning from any native elder who practiced the ancient ways. And he lived his entire life in the American wilderness. Grandfather's life spanned from Ulysses S. Grant to Richard M. Nixon. That's a long time, especially for someone as devoted to learning as was Grandfather.

Grandfather met Tom Brown Jr. when he was eighty-three years old. For ten years, from the time Tom was eight until he was eighteen, Grandfather mentored Tom and his friend Rick (the last few years just with Tom). Today, at 53, Tom is arguably the nation's foremost survivalist expert. He has himself spent extended periods of time wandering North America and shares his experience in over 17 books. He founded and directs The Tracker School in the Pine Barrens of Central New Jersey[51]. He is involved in high profile tracking cases. Students come from all over the world to learn of the

---

[51] **www.trackerschool.com** For those who cannot make the journey to New Jersey, there is an excellent home study course offered by Jon Young, the Kamana Program. Jon was Tom Brown's first student and directs the Wilderness Awareness School in Washington.

skills Grandfather taught Tom. What do they learn? They learn to live with the earth and to thrive in the wilderness. But more than that, they learn a philosophy that enables them to share in the whole reality that is the creation. A central tenet of this philosophy is that we humans are called to be caretakers of the earth.[52] We no longer approach the natural world as a resource to be exploited but as a gift to be treasured and through this perspective we live as grateful children of the earth cared for by the Creator.

You see the common thread in all of this is that the Creator is benevolent. First, as René has pointed out, Jesus' renunciation of retribution is consonant with his vision of God's rule. Jesus' renounces the juxtaposition of God and violence. As we have demonstrated on our site, this has profound consequences for our theology, ethics and worship. Second, as Barth has observed, the intimate connection between creation and covenant means that there is benefit that comes our way in the creation, in our humanness. That benefit is the benevolence of the covenant expressed as creation. And third, following Grandfather is the development of a creation consciousness, of the oneness that is our world that we may celebrate the One who creates us, gives us the Spirit and calls us all children.

---

[52] As Europeans came to the shores of this beautiful continent and as they made their way west, they constantly marveled at the wide range and diverse forms of environments they encountered. It was so beautiful from sea to shining sea because the Native Americans had been cultivating it for over 12,000 years. Kat Anderson (quoting R.F. Heizer and A.B. Elasser) says, "The California Indians were highly accomplished practical botanists, perhaps as knowledgeable about subtle differences in form, color, and behavior as some university professors who have spent their adult lives reading and making field observations. But they were also knowledgeable in a different way – a way directed at understanding nature in such a manner as to use it without destroying it." "Native Californians as Ancient and Contemporary Cultivators" in *Before the Wilderness: Environmental Management by Native Californians*. Thomas Blackburn and Kat Anderson (Menlo Park: Ballena Press, 1993).

Practice of the ancient skills has an added benefit. It is like an insurance policy. They will allow one to survive apart from the economic system if that is one's choice. I have often wondered how Jesus survived apart from the economic system (that craftiest deception of the Powers). I am not satisfied by the explanation that wealthy women supported him. I suspect that Jesus had a comfort zone in the natural world that he could take care of himself with his knowledge and skills, whatever they might have been.[53] The generosity of the women would have been an essential support for the other mouths especially the Twelve. Some might object that Jesus had no contact with those who practiced ancient skills, but such is not the case. The Dead Sea Scrolls reveal an herbalist's awareness of plant life and it is quite plausible that Jesus, either on his own or through John the Baptist, had some connections to the Essenes.[54] Amazingly there are only four basic skills one need learn to survive in the wilderness. These are the skills related to the sacred order, the skills Grandfather passed down: Shelter, Fire, Water, Food. You can learn them in a week, if you try. Almost every other lesson one learns after that comes back to one of these four elements.

---

[53] Jesus is walking alone one night in the wilderness. It is getting cooler. Does he know how to make a fire? Shall he just he just pull out his Bic or a book of matches? How did he make fire? If he was thirsty do you think he knew how to find water? Wild edibles? When scholars imagine Jesus alone in the wilderness they have a tendency to imagine themselves as civilized humans in the wilderness and so project their own insecurities or else they jump on the 'Jesus was divine' bandwagon and single Jesus out as one with special privilege. Both of these are understandable but incorrect. They fail to take into account Jesus' potential 'shamanistic' (wilderness) background.

[54] James Charlesworth, *Jesus and the Dead Sea Scrolls*. (New York: Doubleday, 1992). See also his essay in *Jesus' Jewishness* (New York: Crossroad, 1991). We might also note here Morton Smith's research placing Jesus in the category of 'magician.' In the 18th and 19th centuries it was more common for clergy and theologians to be naturalists and so literature from that period also reflected the romantic relationship civilized humanity had with the natural world. I got news for you: the honeymoon is over.

It does not seem then far-fetched to me to perceive Jesus this way. Jesus' overwhelming preference for nature analogies in describing the Father's kingdom should already indicate to us that he spends time with the creation[55]. This is expected behavior of a shaman. In the gospels he spends a lot of time in the wilderness. It is in the natural world that Jesus is able to perceive the goodness of the Creator, the beneficence of the love of Israel's covenant God, the one whom he called 'daddy.'

One of the real rewards of learning at the feet of Grandfather is that we are taking a journey back in time. We learn the physical skills that our human ancestors used for millions of years as they evolved and came to know the benefits of creation. The contemporary knowledge and practice of these skills puts us in a unique place vis-à-vis our ancestors, since we bring to these skills a more fully developed consciousness[56]. This next section reflects my personal experience of this inter-relation between modern consciousness and pre-civilized awareness. Been there, done that, got the buckskin. Thought I'd tell you about it. The upshot is a new appreciation for the creation and the Creator, the same reason we have gathered here.

---

[55] Michael Goulder argues that Matthew is a liturgical midrash on Mark and has a fascinating chapter on Jesus' (Matthew's) use of natural phenomena as analogies in *Midrash and Lection in Matthew* (London: SPCK, 1974).

[56] Perhaps what I am seeking to do in this next section is well expressed by Eugene Webb *Philosophers of Consciousness* (Seattle: University of Washington Press, 1988): "Unless a way can be found to make sense of the idea of the new life in Christ in a way that is neither objectivistic nor subjectivistic there will be no possibility of hearing the liberating truth Girard thinks the Gospel expresses. One of the rare figures in the Christian tradition who has not only addressed this issue but has made its paradox the center of his own philosophical reflections on human subjectivity, is...Søren Kierkegaard." See also my essay *Reflections on the Spirituality of Soren Kierkegaard* published in The Scottish Journal of Theology Vol. 45, 325-340.

For me, being one with the earth is nothing less and nothing more than honoring all that has been made. It is the embracing of the natural world as a gift, freely given, as from a Father's or Mother's hand, given in love. This shift of perception is the essential element. It is a real shift. The discipline of Ecopsychology has begun to study what happens to people when they are out of doors. There are changes that occur on a physical level, an emotional level, and a spiritual level. Their studies indicate what is called 'the wilderness effect.'[57]

And here is what I have discovered for myself: I have found in the wilderness that I am constantly stripping off layers of false comfort on all levels. The wilderness does that. It helps differentiate between want and need. I may want my warm cozy bed in my nice cozy house but all I need is a debris hut or a scout pit to stay plenty warm and dry, and thus alive. I may want pizza and beer but find that the earth provides me with plenty of trailside edibles and thus meets my need. I may need water and find some collecting the early morning dew. What are wants anyway but mimetic desires? The wilderness doesn't give a damn about desire; instead she meets our needs.

In the wilderness you are often alone even if you are with other people but you are never lonely. At a minimum you are there with yourself. The wilderness will bring you face to face with yourself (a sort of interior mimetic doubling) and in so doing catalyzes an integration process. Alongside and through this process a second process is taking place. The wilderness humbles you. The wilderness

---

[57] Theodore Roszak, Mary Gomes and Allen Kanner Eds. *Ecopsychology* (San Francisco: Sierra Book Club, 1995).

does not tolerate ego or arrogance. It will take you as far down the ladder as you need to go in order to get your attention. (I've gotten to know the bottom rung as a good friend)

As I took classes and began developing my skills, I discovered a freedom I had never enjoyed before. In the wilderness it is just me and the wind, me and the sun, me and the night, me and the snow, me and the rain, me and the swamp. The freer I felt the more I began to ask about Jesus' relationship to the creation in the light of Grandfather's philosophy. And then I began musing about the possibilities of discipleship as living in harmony with the creation. I already had an explanation in hand that illumined how we got into such a mess to begin with in mimetic theory. And in mimetic theory I had the roots for developing a positive mimetic model that could envision life in a holistic fashion, a true and real peace.

However, as I look out over the vast corpus of published research on mimetic theory, which I have by no means mastered, I sense a certain lack of hopefulness. So I wish to engage hopefulness from a Christian perspective but one forged and purified in the fires of mimetic theory and the wilderness. Grandfather taught Tom that if something were pure, it would have to work for anybody in the wilderness.

What do we in the civilized world believe regarding our survival? We have secured our futures with real estate, good paying jobs, tenure and retirement plans. We have no worries. We can always find work as long as the economy stays healthy. But what if it doesn't? What if we find ourselves out of work unable to support our families or ourselves? These "what ifs" are more and more of a possibility as we watch mimetic conflicts destabilize the globe. We are at war with each other and in the process we are at war with the planet. There is nothing more unstable than war.

Need a scapegoat? In 1900, the earth sheltered just over a billion people. In a scant hundred years, in the fastest blink of an eye in terms of the life span of the planet, we humans are now around seven billion and growing. Here's a question: how many people can the planet sustain? Here's another question? How many people can the planet sustain if we are all of the American consumer mentality? Is the answer the same? It has taken us less than 200 years to radically alter the nature of the planet.[58] What will this mean for the future of our children and grandchildren?

For the first time in recorded history scientists have begun to put timetables on the earth's supposedly unlimited resources. We have found that the earth is rapidly losing its ability to sustain such a large population of humans. We have brought the pollution that has poisoned our waters, burned our skies and tarnished our soils. We are the species that has brought a multitude of other species to extinction. We are the species strip-mining the skin of the earth, stripping her by deforestation, and pumping all kinds of deadly toxins through her bloodstream. If we were to do to a human being what we do to the earth, we would be arrested, charged and convicted of murder in the first degree. Not only is God a scapegoat, as we have observed in both mimetic theory and Christian theology, but the creation is also the target of our wrath. We have not learned our lesson. We still think we are like the gods. Humanity in our self-

---

[58] Bill McKibben, *The End of Nature* (New York: Doubleday, 1990).

exaltation commits the basest form of idolatry. What then must we learn in order to escape the vicious circle of our mimetic spiritualities?

One of the most valuable lessons to be learned in the wilderness is the exact same lesson taught by Jesus with regard to discipleship, viz., it's all about surrender. Surrender is not a theological category and we are loath to use it. Too many of us are still enmeshed in a theology of glory, a theology that needs a *deus ex machina*, a powerful savior. We believe that a powerful God will make us powerful. And our spiritualities are just displays of this belief. Our spiritualities are mimetically conceived. On the other hand, a positive mimetic spirituality is characterized by surrender.

When we listen to the Spirit, the One that moves in the world of the creation is also moving in our interior world as well. In the same way that we must surrender to the creation in order to be able to be led in it, so we too must also surrender to the Spirit-that-moves-within-us. This surrender can be described as a complete trust, a giving over, as a setting aside of our egos. It involves developing awareness of what Paul Ricoeur might call our 'fault', that is, the mimetically conceived self[59]. Surrender is the ultimate expression of love not only in relation to humans but also in relation to the creation. In a sense, it is a theology of the cross applied to our experience of creation in both

---

[59] *The Symbolism of Evil* (Boston: Beacon Press, 1967).

its human and non-human aspects[60]. It is to begin to know the Creator as Jesus, Barth and Grandfather knew the Creator, as a benevolent non-retributive loving Other. It is to be fully human.

The Church has tried to neuter Jesus by absorbing his humanity into his divinity.[61] We, who are not divine, really have no chance to be like him. The gospels do not make this mistake. The whole point of telling the story of his life was because we are given such a possibility in the light of God's vindication of this human, who he was, how he lived. And the proof of this was the gift of the Holy Spirit in his name.

Eugene Bianchi writes about the ecological challenge to Christianity and explores a number of recent writers who have contended that ecology is central to Christian spirituality. Bianchi writes,

---

[60] The initial book that helped me make the important connection between suffering and clear trinitarian thought is Arthur McGill's *Suffering: A Test Case of Theological Method* (Philadelphia: Westminster, 1982). It was solidified as I read Jurgen Moltmann *The Crucified God* (New York: Harper & Row, 1974) and Eberhard Jüngel *God as the Mystery of the World* (Grand Rapids: Eerdmans, 1983).

[61] Over the past 200 years biblical scholarship has in various ways tried to address the issue of Jesus' spirituality. Most of the time they suggest it is impossible to gain any access to Jesus' 'inner life.' Christian conservatives on the other hand, project back into Jesus' story their own version of piety and then read it out again. In both of these stances, the discernible element that is missing is the humanity of Jesus. The spirituality of Jesus cannot be conceived apart from what he taught. Does what he taught work? It worked for him. I have sought to address this issue head on with my website **www.preachingpeace.org**. On the shift in emphasis from the humanity to the divinity of Jesus in the early church see Joseph Jungmann, *The Place of Christ in Liturgical Prayer* (Staten Island: Alba House, 1965). Jesus' 'christology', spirituality, ethics and eschatology are all of one piece.

191

"the greatest deficiency in Christian nurture today in most churches is their almost total neglect of cultivating our mystical potential...Few [Christians] have the sense of a personalized path that can be enhanced by regular meditation and other spiritual methods. Institutional religion in the west has generally been suspicious of mysticism because it is hard to control."[62]

The West has little room for the Spirit. This is why Western Christian theology has not been successful in articulating Christology. The realm of the Spirit is not quantifiable and the Church loses its authority in the realm of the Spirit for this is the place we are "all taught by God." The growth of the Pentecostal and charismatic traditions globally have sought to fill this lack in the Western tradition. Unfortunately much of what passes for 'spiritual' in these movements is oriented to Western models of success, marketing, hype and might easily be understood as phenomena related to auto-suggestion, group hypnosis, mass hysteria, etc.

A genuine theology of the Holy Spirit will be cruciform (following the hermeneutic of the Fourth Gospel), egalitarian (following the ecclesiology of the apostle Paul), oriented to liberation manifested not only in terms of healing but also in terms of politics, economics and sociology (the writer of Luke-Acts). A genuine recovery of the work of the Spirit in our time will be holistic, nurturing, beneficent, and yes, mystical. More so, it will always be Jesus-like. We are all called to be followers of the Creator.

---

[62] Eugene Bianchi, "The Ecological Challenge to Christianity" *New Theology Review*, Feb 1998.

The Creator can personally mentor each of us[63]. Imagine that. There are many ways this occurs to us all of the time in the natural world if we will just pay attention.

The wilderness, as I have mentioned, teaches a new perspective on spirituality. Let me give you one example. How many times have you been in the woods and not seen any animals? They are there, why don't you see them? Would you know where to look? More importantly, would you know how to look? Animals have 'neighborhoods' they don't just wander aimlessly, and they are only really active at certain times of day. But how you see is more important. Most people are aware of their peripheral vision when reminded it is there, but most of the time their eyes are focused in a

---

[63] The language of spirituality may be bold language but it is never exclusive. Part of the problem of the narration of Christian experience has been that it is all too frequently done "from above', from the perspective of an exclusivist 'theology of glory.' In developing a 'hermeneutics of testimony', Paul Ricouer asks about the nature of 'the absolute affirmation of the absolute.' He contrasts the experience of original affirmation with 'divestment.' Of course, I automatically think of a theology of the cross here. The possibilities of positive mimesis are as varied as are those of negative mimesis, but positive mimesis, even or especially in its hermeneutics, will be conditioned by surrender. "Original affirmation has all the characteristics of an absolute affirmation of the absolute, but it will neither be able to go beyond a purely internal act not susceptible of being expressed externally, nor even of being maintained internally. Original affirmation has something of the indefinitely inaugural about it, and only concerns the idea that the self makes of itself. This original affirmation, for a reflexive philosophy, is in no sense an experience. Although numerically identical with real consciousness in each person, it is the act which accomplishes the negation of the limitations which affect individual destiny. It is divestment (*depoullemant*). It is by this 'divestment' that reflection is brought to the encounter with contingent signs that the absolute, in its generosity, allows to appear of itself. This 'divestment' is not only ethical but speculative; it is when the thought of the unconditioned has lost all support in the transcendent objects of metaphysics, when it has renounced all the objectifications that understanding imposes. It is then that the claim of the absolute, reduced to the depth of an act immanent to each of our operations, remains steady for something like an experience of the absolute in testimony" in *Essays on Biblical Interpretation* (Philadelphia: Fortress, 1980).

193

tunnel vision. You can see it everywhere you go. In the wilderness tunnel vision will get you hurt. You must readjust the way you see so that you are seeing the entire 180 degrees in front of you. Funny thing is that this doesn't come naturally at first, it is an attitude that becomes a habit that becomes natural. You chose to develop it. Same thing with your ears. It takes practice to learn how to hear nature's concentric rings in 360 degrees. Most of us are selective listeners because we are daily drowned out by noise. The birds are telling us all of the time what is happening around us. Do we listen? Your feet too must learn how to feel the earth and read the landscape. It takes a conscious choice to retrain the sensory organs but when you do, the creation lights up. This experience Grandfather called awareness.

Awareness in the wilderness is a conscious reality, but it involves the suspension of thoughts. In the wild, thoughts are a distraction. They are just interior noise. If you have ever tried any form of meditation you may have experienced the difficulties of quieting your mind. It seems to have so much to say all of the time, even when we are asleep. We are constantly at its mercy with thoughts that just randomly enter our head. Ever tried to turn it off? Sometimes we say we are 'caught up in a thought' or are 'lost in thought.' These are wilderness metaphors. One gets caught in brambles and one gets lost in the wilderness. When you are in a state of conscious awareness, it is as important to be interiorly aware, as it is to be exteriorly aware. Getting lost in one usually gets you lost in the other.

The fact is, if you stop to analyze your thoughts you will realize you are either thinking about what has happened to you or you are thinking about what will happen to you. Your thoughts are about the past or the potential future. We know we can neither alter the past nor control the future. By acknowledging that there is not a thought that is so important that it cannot wait, we are free to be fully in the present.[64]

Awareness might be called intuitive knowing[65]. In awareness, the self is not a center; it is simply part of all that surrounds it. The self is no more a center than is an oak or a fox. We are all part of a grand and glorious creation that when treated with respect shelters us, feeds us, gives us warmth and slakes our thirst. There are no other necessities. Life is brought up to its basic level. And this is the world full of Spirit because it is not full of negative mimetic desire. You learn how to live with nature and thus with Spirit.[66]

---

[64] The theological work that best captures this is Dietrich Ritschl *Memory and Hope: An Inquiry Concerning the Presence of Christ* (New York: Macmillan, 1967). Ritschl shows in what specific ways the ancient and Reformation christological discussions have been hampered by Augustinian dualistic presuppositions. He also argues that these same questions, in different form, have entered the realm of scientific theology in both theology and biblical studies. The upshot is that the Church is called to live between memory and hope where the Christus praesens dwells, that is, fully in the present or in a state of awareness with regard to the Lord.

[65] Bernard Lonergan captures some what occurs in the state of awareness in his Insight. I am not aware of any Native American influence on Lonergan.

[66] Tom Brown Jr. has written an introduction to Grandfather's philosophy, *Awakening Spirits* (New York: Berkley, 1994). But it should be stressed that awareness is only one side of the coin. The external dimension of awareness is tracking. There have never existed better trackers than the Apache. The Apache identified over 4,500 pressure releases that can occur in a track. When I arrived back home from the Advanced Tracking and Awareness class it was as if little light bulbs were everywhere on the lawns and in the gardens of my neighborhood. Tom has explored the first six pressure release studies, about 800 pressure releases in *The Science and Art of Tracking* (New York: Berkley, 1999). It is the only book on tracking that I am aware of that deals with the Apache system of pressure releases (contrast e.g., the fine book by Richard Smith *Animal Signs and Tracking* (Harrisburg: Stackpole, 1982)). For every philosophical skill Grandfather taught that there is a corresponding physical skill as in the combination awareness/tracking or invisibility/camouflage.

We have learned an awful lot about the human brain and the human mind this past 100 years. We have also learned about the importance of right and left-brain inter-connectedness. Unfortunately, psychology, theology and science have all seemingly joined forces to keep them apart. For example, I think Jung's concern was that Freud interpreted the non-conscious *in malem partem*. Jung couldn't do that. He saw something positive at work in the human soul (even if it was some sort of eternal dualism explored as a conjunction of opposites). The Church, of course, has its doctrines of original sin and total depravity, its mortifications, self-flagellations and intellectual taboos.[67] And Science has exalted the left brain and logic and reason to a disastrous dominance and theology has followed right down the line like mice after the Pied Piper. If we are such a rational species why are we killing the planet and ourselves in the process? And consider this: most of us only use about 10% of our total brain capacity. What's the rest for?

In terms of positive mimesis, one is given the option to interpret right brain awareness *in bonum partem*. In the wilderness, this awareness would be called a sixth sense, but it is more accurately described as a precognition of the total input being received by the five senses. In order for this to occur the left brain must be shut off. Neuro Lingustics has taught us that we are limited in our consciousness. Consciousness is a selective activity of the brain. All our senses are

---

[67] These are nothing more than the disastrous results of dualism. Paul Davies *God and the New Physics* (New York: Simon & Schuster, 1983) referring to the influence of dualism on the history of Christianity says, "Central to religious doctrine is the idea that the soul (or mind) is a *thing*, and a sharp distinction must be drawn between the body and the soul. This so-called dualist theory of the mind (or soul) was developed by Descartes and has been widely incorporated in Christian thinking. Indeed, so ingrained in our culture and language are the ideas of dualism that Gilbert Ryle in his book *The Concept of Mind* calls it 'the official doctrine.'"

registering tens of thousands of different impressions a second. We would be on serious overload to be consciously aware of everything we sense. Go look at someone's desk for only three seconds. Turn your back and name everything you can recall seeing. Most of us have recall in the single digits. Now go back and look at what you 'missed.' Your right brain saw everything and under hypnosis you could name everything present, your left brain can only handle small portions or 'bytes' of the picture. Our ROM is not all that large.

In a state of awareness, your mind is sorting all of this sensory data but the data is not sent as a thought, as a form of discourse. In a state of conscious awareness, the mind communicates through emotion. It is a sort of like an internal gyroscope or guidance system. Our intuitive emotion is not, however, alone. In Native American beliefs, all creation shares in the Spirit-that-moves-in-all-things. We are as created as the rocks and the plants so we also share in the Spirit-that-moves-in-all-things. This is neither panentheism nor pantheism. The creation is not deified anymore than we are when God breathed the Spirit into Adam and he became a living being. To be spiritually aware is to share in all of the benefits of being part of God's good creation. It is to share in the joy of the Spirit-that-moves-in-all-things.

In short, anywhere you go in the created realm, you encounter the Creator, whether it is in the natural environment or the wilderness of your soul. When the two become one, then a marvelous reality occurs, and we discover our fundamental oneness with the earth and the Spirit. There is no lost here, there is no hungry, no thirsty, no fatigue and no danger. There is safety, peace, hope, joy and love; in short what the Apostle Paul would call the "fruit of the Spirit." To touch and be touched by this oneness is indeed a privilege.

Our oneness with the creation is not a metaphysical construct, nor is it an idealistic premise. It is the adoption of a positive mimetic posture. Christian theology can take a powerful cue from this orientation. First, by rejecting any notion of retribution in God, one is no longer forced to try and make economic distinctions in the persons of the Trinity, as though God were divided. Second, by removing retaliation from any notion of divine so-called justice, we are then free to follow Jesus as bearers of God's Spirit and believe that the Creator is beneficent. That is, we may actually behave as children of the Creator and thus bring the blessings of the Creator to others and the Earth. This has nothing to do with moral earnestness or religious piety, but purely with the peace that comes from a unified perspective.[68] Third, the Church may also eliminate the category 'wrath of God' from nature. Instead of relating to nature as an enemy, we may find that the reconciliation that Jesus brings also puts us in a right relationship to the creation; the natural world can be our dearest friend.

---

[68] It is rare to find a unitary perspective in theology. I have been quite influenced in this area by Thomas Torrance and John Polkinghorne. See Torrance's *Christian Theology and Scientific Culture* (New York: Oxford University Press, 1981); *Theological Science* (New York: Oxford, 1969); *Space, Time & Incarnation* (New York: Oxford, 1969); *Space, Time & Resurrection* (Grand Rapids: Eerdmans, 1976); *Theology in Reconstruction* (Grand Rapids: Eerdmans, 1975); *Theology in Reconciliation* (Grand Rapids: Eerdmans, 1975); *The Christian Frame of Mind* (Colorado Springs: Helmers & Howard, 1989). By Polkinghorne see *Belief in God in an Age of Science* (New Haven: Yale, 1998); *Faith, Science & Understanding* (New Haven: Yale, 2000); *The God of Hope and the End of the World* (New Haven: Yale, 2002). The implications of quantum mechanics are just beginning to filter into theology and social science. There is an interesting discussion of quantum mechanics in relation to social science in Menas Kafatos and Robert Nadeau, *The Conscious Universe: Part and Whole in Modern Physical Theory* (Springer-Verlag, 1990).

There is then a double lens that must be used in reading the gospels if one is to fully appreciate them. The tool is mimetic theory; the stereo-opticon effect is created by viewing both negative mimesis and its effects side by side with positive mimesis and its effects. This is precisely what the gospels do.

Mimetic theory puts the delusory stance of scientific 'assured results' on notice. Science has not made the world a better place, it has destroyed it. Mimetic theory also illumines Christian theology by virtue of the role the gospel plays within René Girard's appropriation of mimetic theory. Other mimetic theorists may well diverge from Girard here and for good reason.[69] Christian theology and church life stink of far too many wrong questions and answers. But Girard is correct to also apply mimetic theory to the Gospels. In so doing, the heart of human civilization is exposed and so is God's.

I have also said that positive mimesis has implications for all levels of our human existence. This is a consequence of my understanding of the doctrine of the Incarnation. In Jesus, God fully assumes our humanness so that we may fully share in Jesus' relationship with the Creator. This is what the New Testament calls the gift of the Holy Spirit, that is, to be spiritually aware. It is not about religion, it is about the way creation is perceived and creation perceive as apart

---

[69] E.g., Lucien Scubla, "The Christianity of René Girard and the Nature of Religion" in Paul Dumouchel, ed., *Violence and Truth: On the Work of René Girard* (Stanford: Stanford University Press, 1985). In contrast, a more positive appreciation of Girard's appropriation of biblical texts within the framework of the scapegoat theory can be found in the article by Aidan Carl Mathews, "Knowledge of Good and Evil: The Work of René Girard" in *To Honor René Girard* (Saratoga: ANMA Libri & Co, 1986).

from the Spirit is a poor, dark, dreary place indeed.[70]

All of us are standing by while the planet is dying and whether Jewish, Christian, Buddhist, Hindi, Muslim or anything else, it is the creation of our Creator that we are killing. We are all in this thing together. History will ask why we did nothing to stop it. Future decimated generations writing their dissertations (assuming things don't turn into some Mad Max scenario) may well wonder why we didn't see it coming? How blind could we have been? It is not apocalyptic speculation to say that the world is primed for some pretty major ecological crises in the current century. Maybe not in your lifetime, but in the lifetime of your children and grandchildren this is a virtual certainty.

I believe it is possible not only to do good theology but also to live in peace. My concerns about the planet are addressed to Christians, the tradition in which I was raised. Others are free to eavesdrop as they wish. If the Church is to have any effect in the twenty-first century, let us hope that it will begin to address the issue of the relationship of following Jesus to the Earth, which, after all, we confess was made through Him. Just imagine what might happen should a billion Christians care for the Earth and all her children and every creature as the most important part of their spirituality.

---

[70] Christologically speaking, George A.F. Knight, *Christ the Center* (Grand Rapids: Eerdmans, 1999) concludes that the very earth itself, the creation which sustained Jesus is transformed in the resurrected body of Jesus. "We are left with the inference that Jesus in his person was now the first fruits of the new nature, the new cosmos, and as well as being such, victor over the powers of evil." Jesus' resurrection is the eschatological healing of the creation.

So then, what happens when you sit down with a French historian, a Swiss theologian and an Apache shaman? You see a heart gripping vision of the way things are and how they came to be groaning here amidst darkness but at the same time you see a hopeful new vision of light and the way things can be.

Does mimetic theory have anything to contribute to the environment and environmental studies? You bet it does!

Made in the USA
Charleston, SC
07 April 2016